# Coaching for Behavior Change

✦

## A Practical, Easy to Use 5-Step Method

*Jack Scannell, MA*
*Founder of Esteem Therapy,*
*Certified Reality Therapist,*
*Certified Chemical Dependency Counselor*

iUniverse, Inc.
New York   Bloomington

# Coaching for Behavior Change

## A Practical, Easy to Use 5-Step Method

iUniverse books may be ordered through booksellers or by contacting:

iUniverse
1663 Liberty Drive
Bloomington, IN 47403
www.iuniverse.com
1-800-Authors (1-800-288-4677)

ISBN: 978-0-595-45899-8 (pbk)
ISBN: 978-0-595-50913-3 (cloth)
ISBN: 978-0-595-90199-9 (ebk)

Printed in the United States of America

# *Dedication*

This book is dedicated to all of the children, adults, and families that I was so fortunate to be able to serve in my programs. It is also dedicated to everyone using the methods described herein for improvement in personal development or functioning.

# Contents

# *Acknowledgments*

I want to acknowledge and thank the teaching staff members of the Chemical Dependency Counseling Program at the Rio Salado College, and the special instruction and certification staff at the Reality Therapy Institute in Phoenix, AZ for their competent instructional courses, training and insights. I also give special thanks to Dr. William Glasser, founder of Reality Therapy. During many of my treatment activities, as well as the general development of the Esteem Therapy model, I often borrowed heavily from his training and model.

I have special thanks and appreciation to Nick Saldana, the State of AZ Substance Abuse Program Coordinator for his encouragement to propose my Esteem Therapy model to the State of AZ for the Corrections Department contract activities. I also want to thank Drs. Allan Price and Joselyn Fuller, supervising psychologists at various AZ Department of Corrections institutions during my extensive Substance Abuse contract activities, for their important reviews, discussions, encouragement and recognition regarding the applications using the Esteem Therapy model for treatment of very difficult cases.

For the excellent contract support given to me during my extensive activities for the AZ Department of Economic Security - Child Protective Services Division, I wish to thank my contract administrator, Laurie White and her staff. Also, in Northern AZ, I wish to thank all of the staff in the various local Child Protective Services offices for their referrals and support.

I want to thank my fellow authors, Dr. Charles A. Cummins and my daughter, Dr. Denise Scannell, for their helpful editing suggestions during the preparation of this book.

During the three years that I authored the weekly newspaper column, entitled **Family Forum**, I had the unique opportunity to communicate and interact in print with a large residential readership. I want to thank all of those readers for their enthusiastic response to that column. I also want to thank the Community Human Services non-profit agency in Upstate NY for allowing me to serve on their Board of Directors and participate in their "**Meet the Author**" series at that same point in time.

Finally, I want to thank and express my profound appreciation to the many children, adults and families who actively participated in my different treatment programs. Without you, this book would not have been possible.

# *Foreword*

Theory sometimes has a hard time finding its way into practice - especially in education. That's why I was interested when Jack Scannell first described to me his 5-STEP program of *Coaching for Behavior Change* in children and other populations. He had taken a theory and transformed it into a practice.

This is no simple task. I know. While studying for my doctorate, research led me to investigate a number of theories that somehow never got off the drawing board. They looked and sounded good but no one ever put them into practice with real children. I knew there was some good research going on in education that most people would never hear about.

This led me to start writing my weekly newspaper column called *Report Card on Education*. In it I tried to share with parents some of the news about education from behind the scenes, so to speak. Jack Scannell came to me because of something he read in one of my columns. That column concerned a letter from a father who was looking for help in handling his 12-year-old daughter. She was, in his words, obsessed with her looks. "She spends every waking minute in front of the mirror," he wrote. His letter told me that she did not spend a lot of time watching television or talking with girlfriends, nor did she presently show much interest in boys.

At this point you might think, as I did, that she was a typical pre-teen, caught in that awkward stage between girlhood and womanhood. Later in his letter he explained that she was diagnosed as emotionally disabled by her school and attended special classes, where academic progress was slow. She did most of her homework at school, under the direction of the special education teacher, so she had little school work to do at home.

He had found some success working with her in her piano lessons that consisted of step-by-step instructions. He asked if I knew of any program he and his wife could use that would guide them step-by-step in dealing with their daughter's behavior. They desperately wanted to help her but, so far, had been unable to get much help from the school of anyone else. They got a lot of theory, but little practical advice.

I knew of no step-by-step program they could use. So I made an appeal to my readers. "Somewhere among my readers," I wrote, "maybe someone who has knowledge of a book or other material that will provide step-by-step lessons for dealing with one obsession, one behavior problem, one personal problem or one social problem at a time." That's when Jack called and asked if I would be interested in seeing a program he had used successfully during the time he coordinated a program for troubled youth in Arizona. I agreed to meet with him and, as they say, the rest is history. You have the results of that meeting in your hands.

Study these five steps. Learn them and use them exactly as Jack has outlined them. This is a step-by-step manual for dealing with almost any long-term or repeating behavior problem - allowing, of course, for variations due to age and circumstance. This is theory made into practice.

*Coaching for Behavior Change* is an action manual. You can put it to work for you immediately. I am sure you will have success.

Charles A Cummins, Ed.D.

# *Author's Note*

From the mid-1980s to mid-'90s, I had the opportunity to serve populations with special needs as a contract therapist in the State of Arizona. I initially began this activity with multiyear contracts from the AZ Department of Juvenile Corrections for applying my own unique model of **Esteem Therapy** for substance abuse treatment of the incarcerated children, both in the institution and, later, with their families in the community. This model is based on the basic premise that recovery from any dysfunctional state is not possible without some minimum level of self-esteem. The Esteem Therapy methodology focuses on providing that minimum level.

Applications of this model, both in the institution and community resulted in unprecedented success in terms of rates of recovery and reduced institutional recidivism. All of the cases treated in the institution were very closely monitored because of the security issues, and once the persons left the institution to reintegrate back into the family and community, there was still a high degree of monitoring and case accountability. So, it was possible to consider this program for the AZ DOC as a "study" in the sense that the environment was restricted and monitoring of behaviors was constant and complete by institution and community probation staff. Thus, the outcome, i.e. changes as a direct result of my treatment model, were viewed as meaningful by both State administrators and staff.

The results of this study were written in a detailed report that was subsequently published by the author and distributed to the appropriate departments in all 50 of the United States. Since this report were never made available to the general public, and because the historical basis for Esteem

Therapy and the use of **Coaching** in conjunction with Esteem Therapy is contained in this report, it has been  included in this text as Appendix A for reference and additional information about the model for the interested reader and professionals.

Following the unprecedented success with this population, I proposed and was awarded multiyear contracts to provide psychological treatment services using the same Esteem Therapy model for the special populations involved with the Child Protective Services Division and the Developmental Disabilities Division of the Arizona Department of Economic Security. That contract activity also resulted in unprecedented successes for helping dysfunctional families achieve a higher level of functioning and parenting that would, in turn, allow children "at risk" to remain in the home.

Finally, before returning to private practice, I had the opportunity to serve as a contract therapist for the State of Arizona Supreme Court, and the Adult Probation Department of Coconino County of Arizona with similar success rates for these populations.

After providing successful private and contractual services to thousands of children, adults and families using the Esteem Therapy model with Coaching as an important tool, I decided to publish the method in a way that could be used by anyone for achieving improved self-esteem and behavior change. Therefore, it is not my intention that this book can only be understood and used by professional caregivers.  Of course, it should be highly useful to that group also, especially those working in an institutional setting.

A major goal in producing this book was to give parents, coaches, and other non-professionals interested in behavior change, a proven and practical method that can be used by anyone-regardless of education or experience. After many years of working in this arena, I know that most people have a very practical, "cut-to-the-chase," attitude about books of this type and really want a simple, step-by-step approach.  Unlike the professionals, parents and coaches are usually not interested in plowing through boring details about the theories involved. They simply want to know what works and how it can be used now!

Therefore, to satisfy their wants and interests *Coaching for Behavior Change* primarily focuses on the method and how it is actually used. Except for a few key concepts, each chapter presents, in everyday language that is easy to understand, practical "how-to" information about the five steps used in the method, along with some common examples introduced as case studies. A brief chapter overview is presented below.

The Introduction contains new ideas and universals that need to be understood before going to the separate steps in the following chapters. Using very common case study examples with children, behaviors are discussed in terms of behavior **standards** and a unique **map**. An overview description of the map is given, and map **Points A and B** are defined.

Chapter 1 is **Step 1: What Are They Doing?** This is **Point A** on the behavior map where the person is operating before they change. The behaviors of one of the children discussed in the Introduction is used for the example. This example will be continued throughout the book to illustrate the method on a detailed practical level.

Chapter 2 is **Step 2: What Should They be Doing?** The focus in this chapter helps the coach learn to identify the behaviors expected in a situation and to separate it into small sections. This is **Point B** on the map.

Chapter 3 is **Step 3: Comparing Behavior Lists and Choices.** The breakdown of the two behaviors is compared to identify needed change and the new choices available to the person.

Chapter 4 is **Step 4: Preparing the Person for Change.** This is the important initial contact with the person prior to any behavior trials. A proven script of key questions and dialog is given for the coach to follow.

Chapter 5 is **Step 5: Traveling from Point A to Point B.** This chapter focuses on precisely what must be done to help the person make changes in a step-by-step method from Point A to Point B. A detailed script for giving feedback is provided and plays a very important role in this step, and in the total process for achieving and maintaining successful change.

Chapter 6 is a **Summary** of the complete method and is given using a new case study in which a parent with a problem child has been trained to successfully use the method described in this book.

In Chapter 7, **Variations** using the method are addressed.

Chapter 8, **Helping the Person Stay at Point B**, focuses on helping the person maintain the behavior changes over long periods of time. The concept of relapse and relapse prevention are discussed as important issues here.

Chapter 9, **Method Example: Tiffany's Tantrums**, uses a typical example for applying the complete method by a parent trained to coach her young child for behavior changes.

Finally, Chapter 10, **Postscript: The Model,** presents a brief overview of the model, including the primary influences for each of the steps.

Appendix A contains the report, entitled "**Results of the Esteem Therapy Substance Abuse Treatment Model for Juvenile Offenders**" in its entirety, including letters of program observation and recommendations by significant State of AZ Department of Corrections staff. In this appendix, the Esteem Therapy model is described, along with the important role and applications of Coaching. This complete document is included here to provide additional background information for the interested reader, and to be available as a resource tool for professionals working in institutional settings with similar populations.

Although the 5-Step method described here <u>could</u> be used for any type of behavior problem, it is not intended for use with someone who occasionally makes inappropriate, or bad choices of behavior - because everyone does that from time-to-time. It is primarily designed for interrupting and correcting **patterns** of inappropriate behavior that could seriously affect the person's overall functioning and/or development in the long term.

An additional goal in writing this book was to give parents, coaches and others some proven effective tools for problems that they could manage without having to call upon professionals. I take this point of view after visiting and working with thousands of families who really could have solved their own problems if they only had the right tool. I am confident that *Coaching for Behavior Change* is that tool!

Although there are behaviors that cannot be altered, or corrected with this method, its application with any problem certainly will never exacerbate the situation, because - bottom line- the person's self esteem will be improved as a result of such exposure. For behaviors that this method cannot change successfully, professional consultation, ultimately, may be necessary. However, in this case, having applied the 5-STEP method of *Coaching for Behavior Change* beforehand is very likely to reduce the person's time in such treatment.

# *Introduction*

## The Behavior Map

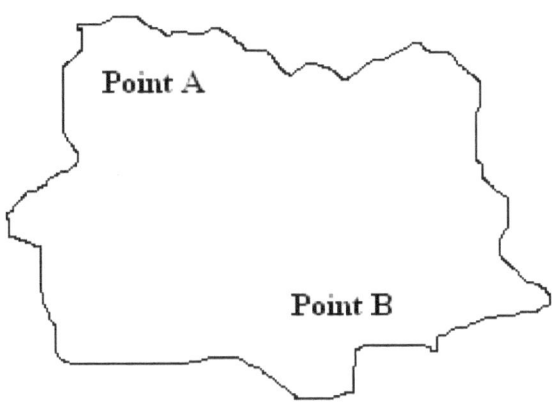

*A good map is invaluable for traveling
from Point A to any new Point B.*

### Example Problem Behaviors

The examples given below for some typical problems are based on real cases referred  by the State of Arizona, Department of Economic Security - Child Protective Services Division and the State of Arizona, Department of Economic Security - Developmental Disabilities Division during my contract periods 5/18/89 - 6/30/92 and 7/1/92 - 6/30/94. Although these examples, and much that is discussed in this book, specifically focus on my work with children and their families, the method described here is not solely limited to those populations. As mentioned previously, **Appendix A** provides additional information from work with a different population.

Jason acted like a normal 18-month-old, except for his exploration of feelings during play. Whenever feelings of anger or aggression were involved, he stopped all activities and cried until held. At his age, he was **expected** to explore these kinds of negative feelings in more understandable ways, like violently crashing his cars, or by having his toy figures beat up each other, etc.

Tiffany was the 4-year-old of a divorced working mother forced to leave her at a nursery every weekday. She frequently threw tantrums, leaving everyone drained for the remainder of the day. Tiffany's difficulties with the daily separation were understandable, however, at her age she was **expected** to have some capacity to cope.

Janine was a 7 -year-old without friends at school, or home. During brief interactions with peers, her bossy behavior always resulted in such conflict and anger that no one would play with her. Wanting to do things her way was not surprising, but she was **expected** to negotiate and compromise.

As a 15-year-old, Daniel often acted impulsively during stressful situations. During arguments with her parents, she ran away from home for long periods. While some emotional volatility is normal for a 15-year-old, some capacity for self-regulation also was **expected**.

These examples illustrate situations and behaviors that most parents have either experienced or witnessed. At a glance they appear to be different in nearly all ways that can be compared, such as their situations, gender, ages, behaviors, etc. However, they all share in common one significant behavior feature that was highlighted in boldface print - **expected** behaviors for their age in the typical situation described.

## Expected Behaviors - Point B

In the examples given above, some behaviors were emphasized as "expected" of children in each situation. The behaviors expected were not limited to a single way of acting, but a range of ways. For example, Tiffany could have chosen different behaviors that would have been acceptable in her situation. She could have cried for a few minutes to vent feelings and then be nurtured. Other acceptable choices would have been pouting, showing anger, refusing to say goodbye to her mother, etc. While her mother would have still left her, Tiffany would have been viewed as "on track" developmentally because her behaviors would have been in the range expected for her age in that type of situation.

People in all cultures define and use an acceptable range of ways to act in common situations. Those ways are acceptable because they allow getting needs and wants met in those situations without interfering with others trying to do the same. In other words, **expected behaviors** in a culture are the appropriate and effective behaviors that people learn to use for coping, and getting needs and wants met.

Since these ways of acting are accepted and used by most people, they become behavior standards that are expected of everyone. As a result, everyone learns these standards while growing up and living in their culture. Because this observation is so important in the method of coaching for behavior change, it is specifically expressed as a **principle**:

*In every culture, there are expected
behaviors for all common situations.*

The advantage in having such standards is that they can be used to compare and identify important differences. In Tiffany's case, she would have been seen as "on track" in her development had she chosen to act within the range of ways expected. Then, her behaviors would have matched the behaviors expected without a significant difference, or **deviation**.

Another way to explain this concept is to consider the camera. Some cameras come with the capability of focusing using two images before taking a picture. Both images are identical, but are provided during viewing to be precisely lined up to become one. With this type of camera, the best photographic results are achieved when the two images are aligned with each other so that, when compared through the viewfinder, one is exactly superimposed over the other so that there is no difference between the two. This is the situation of best focus for taking a picture. In a similar way, a person's actual behaviors give the best results when their actual behaviors are **aligned**, or are matched as closely as possible with the expected behaviors in common situations.

In this method for coaching to change behaviors, when the behaviors used closely match the expected behaviors, the person is considered to be located at the **Point B** on the special **behavior map**. Thus, by definition, Point B has the significance of being the "standard" for comparing behaviors. This is expressed as in the following principle:

*Point B behaviors are the range of
behaviors expected in most situations.*

In the example used for Tiffany, there was a noticeable deviation between her actual behaviors and the behaviors expected. Having such a large deviation, she certainly would not have been found at Point B. In fact, for Tiffany, Point B behaviors would be a goal achieved only through using the method described here as coaching for behavior change.

## Deviations from Point B

Because everyone is unique, small deviations will always be present, simply as a result of individual style/personality. However, when the difference between a person's behaviors and the expected behaviors is large enough to be notable, it is the size of the deviation that determines the impact in their life, and in their development. In general, the larger the deviation, the greater the developmental impact. If the impact is small enough to be tolerated by others, a person with this type of problem may regularly use behaviors that are simply considered eccentric. In any case, they do not conform to social norms and there can be consequences in their relationships.

When there is a larger deviation between the range of behaviors expected and the behaviors actually used, it may be a more serious problem. In Tiffany's case there was a large deviation between her actions and those expected for her age in the situation described. In addition to the impact her behaviors had on everyone around during her tantrums, it had a potentially significant impact on her life, because instead of being developmentally on-track compared with her peers, she was seen as emotionally delayed and socially dysfunctional. Without correction her behaviors would probably have progressed to the more serious level and labels of "emotionally-handicapped" and "anti-social."

Tiffany's behaviors, and the behaviors of the children in the other examples, deviated greatly from the expected. In practical terms, acting in ways that were far from the expected behaviors meant that her actual behaviors were located at a point that was quite distant from Point B.

If a deviation, *sufficient to affect a person's development/growth*, exists between the actual behaviors and the expected behaviors at **Point B,** the location of the actual/deviant behaviors is defined in this method as **Point A.** Thus, the old cliché term about "getting from Point A to Point B," has very practical significance in this method of coaching for changing behaviors.

## Deviant Actual Behaviors - Point A

The fact that a person's behaviors are occasionally noticeably different compared to the expected, does not always indicate that there is a problem. Short-term deviations from expected behaviors also can be due to some very common causes, including:

1. Random acts of misbehavior

2. Poor judgment in a situation

3. Experimentation/Problem Solving

4. Limit Testing/Challenging

5. Physiological, such as fatigue, sleeplessness, etc.

Most persons having a problem due to some of the common deviations listed above, typically, do not need professional help for making better choices in the future. While growing up, <u>corrective nudges</u> from parents, or others to choose better behaviors in the future were usually all that were necessary for effectively getting these children back on track. In most cases, normal parental correction methods work well with these individuals. As a result, the problem choices are often not repeated, and there are no long-term effects on their development.

Thus, periodic deviations for these reasons are quite normal and happen in the lives of all children while growing up. However, there are important differences between such spontaneous and short-term deviations in behaviors and those that are defined as **Point A**. Some of the differences for Point A behaviors are the following:

- The behaviors are repeated, or become part of a pattern,

- Normal behavioral correction methods are ineffective,

- The behaviors affect the child's development.

While individuals located at Point A may receive the same corrective nudges by parents and others, usually it is to no avail. These persons tend to repeat their troublesome choices and develop a **pattern of behaviors** that become a problem for themselves and others. Point A may now be defined in a general way:

*Point A behaviors are inappropriate and ineffective behaviors for getting needs and wants met, <u>and</u> affect the person's development when used repeatedly.*

With Points A and B generally defined, the **Behavior Map** can now be introduced.

## The Behavior Map
(The earliest use of the concept of applying a map for behavior change by this author is presented in Appendix A.)

Points A and B are **behavior locations** and the **Behavior Map** is simply a visual aid that shows the best path for traveling from behavior Point A to behavior Point B. To be most effective as a map, it should be sufficiently comprehensive to include the behaviors found at those specific points, and everything in between. However, it would be a very busy and complicated map if every possible variation of behavior were included. To keep it simple, a general overview was taken that focused on a single basic question. Since this map was designed to be about places showing behaviors, that question was:

*"Where are the primary places in life that behaviors are used?"*

In other words, in the different areas of all of our human functioning, <u>where</u> are behaviors located? In general, these locations, or places, are **personal** places, **relationship** places and **reality** places (limits, etc.) These are the common areas in everyone's life where behavior choices are constantly and continuously being made. Each of these three general areas includes a *range* of behaviors that include Point A and Point B locations, as well as everything in between.

When a basic behavior map is drawn, these three areas are shown as the sides of a 2-dimensional figure. With only three sides, the only shape this type of map can take is that of a triangular figure. Making the sides equal in length and adding the names, the general map shown in Figure I-1 is produced.

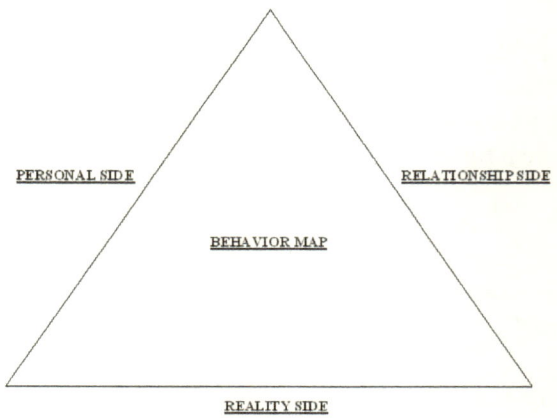

**Figure I-1 Basic map showing the 3 general areas where behaviors are used.**

Each side of this map represents a range of behaviors for that general area and has special features making it easy to locate a person's problem behavior. Each side has a place in the middle, or **midpoint,** showing the most effective and appropriate way of behaving in that range. As may be expected, the further away from the midpoint the behaviors are, the less effective and more problematic the behaviors. By definition in this method of coaching for changing behaviors, persons behaving near the endpoints of a range are functioning in highly ineffective, and possibly "dysfunctional," ways, and may be characterized as having serious developmental problems, or delays.

The location of a general midpoint along a side is shown in Figure I-2.

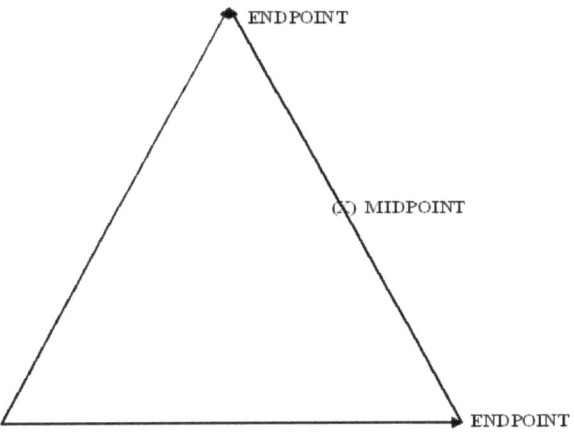

ENDPOINT

(X) MIDPOINT

ENDPOINT

**Figure I-2 Basic map showing the general behavior range.**

Each range will now be described in more specific terms.

The range of behaviors along the **PERSONAL** side includes all actions, thoughts, feelings and physiological responses, i.e. perspiring, tearing, etc. These behaviors are unique to each individual, and when used repeatedly, help to identify each of us as unique. The focus of this side is **regulation,** or how well persons manage the different parts of their total behavior, i.e. actions, thoughts, physiology, and especially, their **emotions.**

The midpoint along the Personal behavior range is defined as "**Self-Regulated.**" Individuals operating near this midpoint have the ability to regulate themselves as needed, yet remain spontaneous enough for responding freely to a variety of sensations and experiences. Such is not the case at the two endpoints on this side.

At the endpoint where the Personal side meets the Reality side, the behaviors are defined as "**IMPULSIVE.**" Individuals found near this endpoint do not regulate themselves adequately in terms of how they cope with external stimuli from the outside world. They often lose control, overreact, or act too spontaneously in situations where it is inappropriate.

At the opposite endpoint extreme, the behaviors are defined as "**INHIBITED**." Individuals located near this endpoint over-regulate their personal behaviors. They lack the ability to respond in free and spontaneous ways. They tend to withdraw rather than interact with the outside world. They are often perceived as shy by others. All these points along the Personal behaviors side of the map are shown in Fig. I-3.

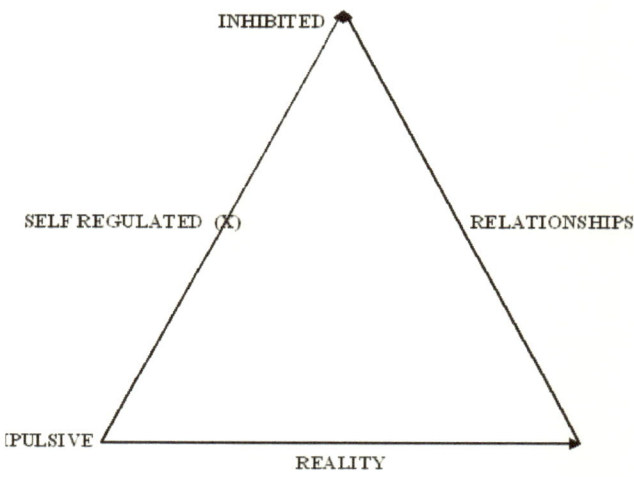

**Figure I-3 Basic map depicting the PERSONAL behavior range.**

The behavior range for the **RELATIONSHIP** side of the map is defined in a similar way. These behaviors are simply all the ways that individuals choose to deal, or interact with others. The focus for this side is their state of dependence on others. The midpoint is defined to be the familiar term, "**INTERDEPENDENT**", and has the same meaning as in the field of psychology. Interdependent behavior is also viewed as relating to others in a balanced way in this method.

As may be expected for this side and focus, the endpoints are about dependency. The endpoint where the Relationship side meets the Reality side is the overly-dependent state defined as "**ENGULFED**." While growing up in most families, individuals continue to have dependency needs for many years. However, the behaviors found near this location affect their development in negative ways. Near this extreme, they tend to merge their lives with those of others, and can approach the highly dysfunctional state of being symbiotic in their relationships with others.

At the opposite end where the Relationship side meets the Personal side, the endpoint is the overly-independent state defined as "**ISOLATED.**" Near this extreme, individuals tend to avoid relationships, be overly independent and may not easily allow others in their lives.

Figure I-4 shows all of these points along the Relationship side.

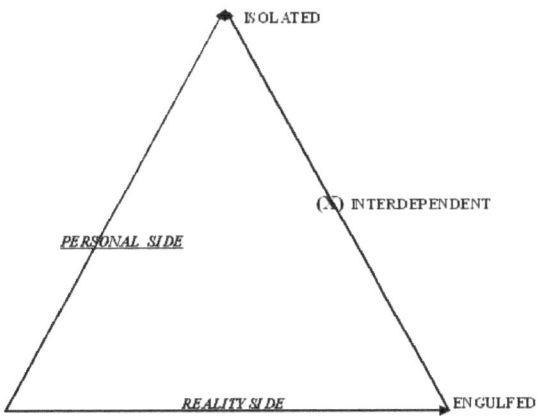

**Figure I-4 Basic map depicting the RELATIONSHIP behavior range.**

The final behavior range to define is along the **REALITY** side of the map. Behaviors found in this range are about how individuals deal with certain issues of reality, including the following:

- limits
- limitations
- expectations
- cause and effect
- how the world works

This side focuses on the person's view of their world, or **Shared Reality,** and of the effects of their behaviors in that world. The midpoint is "**Consensus.**" When the person's behaviors are near this midpoint, their views are closely matched with those of others. In other words, they see things "realistically" because they share the same reality as the rest of the world.

The endpoint where the Reality side meets the Personal side is defined as **"Self-focused."** Children and adults near this extreme location have a view of reality that is very different than the consensus. That view is unrealistic because they see *reality primarily in terms of themselves* and may totally reject the perceptions others have about some things, especially their problem behaviors. Thus, they engage in a form of denial at this extreme.

At the opposite extreme where the Reality side meets the Relationship side, the endpoint is defined as **"Others-focused."** At this end, children, and adults view reality in a different way than the consensus, because they see *reality primarily in terms of the people* involved in their lives. By rejecting their own perceptions they do not join the consensus, but rely on others to mediate reality and make sense of their world for them. The behaviors found at this extreme are another form of denial.

Figure I-5 shows these points along the Reality Side.

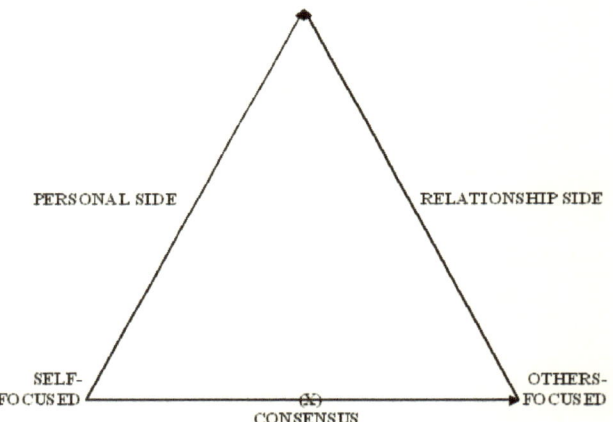

**Figure I-5 Basic map depicting the REALITY behavior range.**

The complete map showing all of the behavior ranges is presented in Figure I-6. It includes the ranges, endpoints and midpoints (identified as (X) on each side.)

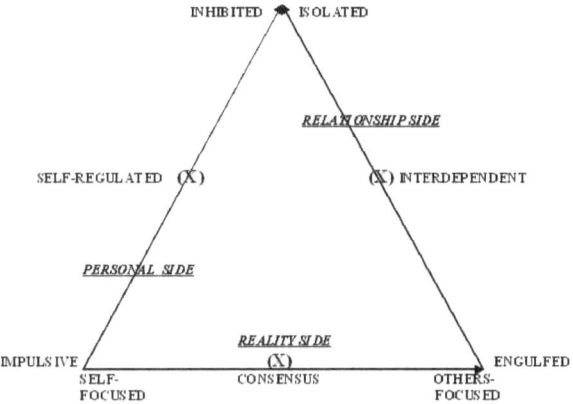

**Figure I-6 Basic map with all behavior ranges, endpoints and midpoints (identified as (X) on each side.)**

To complete the basic behavior map and progress to Step 1 of this method, it is only necessary to show the permanent location of Point B. While Point A will necessarily depend on the person's problem, Point B is always in the same ideal operating area -- at the exact center of the map. There is a very good reason for this location.

The midpoint of each side of the map is where a person's behaviors are most effective in all areas, i.e. personal, relationship, and reality. The only location on the map where it is possible for a person to be found at the midpoint in all three of these areas at the same time is at the center of the triangular figure, or if in 3-dimensions, the center of the pyramid. Thus, the center represents the place where individuals behave in the expected ways that bring, or keep them, **centered,** or in balance with all parts of their lives. Realistically, that ideal state is rarely ever achieved for long periods by children while growing up. As a result, Point B is shown as an <u>area</u> of expected behavior that also has a range. The Point B range is defined by extending lines inward from the midpoints of each side until they meet, or intersect at the center. Figure I-7 shows the lines and that central Point B area where the lines have intersected.

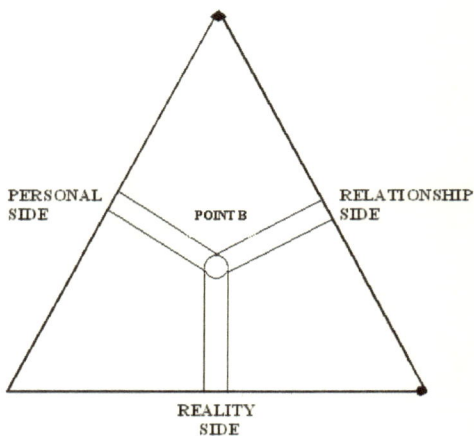

**Figure I-7 The general Behavior Map depicting the midpoints
of each side and the Point B range formed at the
intersection of the midpoints at the center.**

The general Point B behavior map showing some important characteristic features for each side is given below in figure I-8.

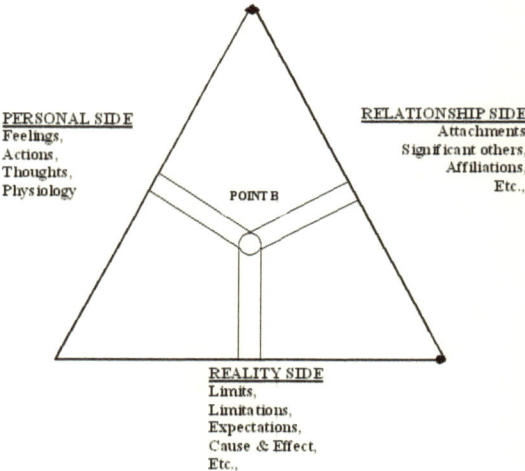

**Figure I-8 The general behavior map showing some important
characteristics for each side.**

Now that the basic concepts have been introduced, the method of coaching for behavior change can be described using the map.

Before proceeding to **Step 1** of this method, the concepts presented in this chapter are summarized as a checklist of key information to understand and remember.

## Chapter Checklist: Things to remember

- Every culture has **expected behaviors** for common situations.

- **Point B** is the range of behaviors expected in most situations.

- When behaviors used in a common situation are not the expected, the difference is a **deviation.**

- The deviation from Point A behaviors affects a person's development when used repeatedly.

- Point A and B Behaviors are found in **Personal, Relationship** and **Reality** places in everyone's lives that can be shown on a behavior map.

- The Personal, Relationship and Reality places of behavior are the sides of the behavior map. Each side has a range, a midpoint area and two endpoints. The midpoints are the expected behaviors, while the endpoints are extreme behaviors along each side.

- The range on the Personal side is focused on regulation, with the midpoint of **self-regulated** and the endpoints of INHIBITED and IMPULSIVE.

- The range on the Relationship side is focused on dependency, with a midpoint of **interdependence** and endpoints of ENGULFED and ISOLATED.

- The range on the Reality side is focused on shared reality, with the midpoint of **consensus**, and endpoints of SELF-FOCUSED and OTHERS-FOCUSED.

- The location of Point B is defined as an area in the exact center of the behavior map for any situation.

- The location of Point A depends upon children's behavior problems in any situation.

# Chapter 1

## *Step 1: What Are They Doing?*

*Before beginning the travel to Point B, one must first have accurate knowledge of the initial location, i.e. Point A.*

In this step-by-step approach to coaching for behavior change, the first step that must always be completed before continuing with the method is to identify what the person is **actually doing.** Since understanding what they are doing in terms of situational behaviors is the key to using this method, at this point it will be discussed how to examine them in sufficient depth, and demonstrate a process for separation of behavior parts, regardless of the behavior complexity.

### Examining Situations

While situations and ranges can be different, the expected behaviors are found in all areas of a person's life. It is important to recognize that the **content** of a situation can include emotions and relationships, as well as tasks. When emotions or relationships are involved, the behavior can be as simple as expressing a basic emotion when someone has been hurt, i.e. sadness, sympathy, etc., or as complex as performing a tragic role in a play before a large audience.

Regardless of content, **expected situational behaviors** are the logical starting point for coaching individuals to make corrections. Regardless of the complexity, such behaviors are first learned by practicing and mastering the small, "manageable" parts of the total behavior, then finally putting the parts together in the right order for it to be performed. From this perspective, the process of correcting situational behaviors can be accomplished by examining each of the small, manageable parts, then correcting those that deviate from the parts that are expected and necessary for successful overall behavior in that situation.

A practical, and very common example of this concept will be helpful. A situational behavior for a typical task, that typically has no emotional content and that everyone must learn is that of hand-washing. Parents can not expect children to intuitively know how to wash their hands if it has always been done for them. They must be helped to acquire these behaviors. This typically involves parents teaching all of the following small parts, somewhat in the order listed.

1.  Go to the sink
2.  Turn on the water
3.  Wet hands
4.  Pick up soap and rub on hands
5.  Put down the soap
6.  Rub hands together
7.  Put hands under water and rinse
8.  Turn off the water
9.  Dry hands on the towel

While there can be additions and variations to this task, the above general list will do the basic job of teaching children how to wash their hands. Young children shown the total behavior for the first time may see the task as overwhelming. However, each small part is easy to understand and to do, and with some practice, they finally are able to perform all in the right order to eventually end up with clean, dry hands - more or less. From that point on, neither children nor parents ever have to think in terms of all of the small separate parts that have been involved each time someone says, "Go and wash your hands for dinner."

Breaking down such situational behaviors into small, easy-to-do/manageable parts is an unwritten and informal task and skill for most parents. It is one that they are usually not even consciously aware. It should be mentioned that the skill generally has only been used with task types of behaviors that have no emotional content. However, depending upon the

**feedback** given for this task, and many other basic tasks, emotional and relationship content can often be involved. The importance of giving the right kind of feedback will be addressed in later chapters.

In this 5-STEP method of *Coaching for Behavior Change*, this basic approach is used as a practical coaching tool that can be expanded to include behaviors that typically <u>do</u> contain emotional and relationship content! (The earliest use of the concept of Coaching with a therapeutic modality by the author is found in Appendix A.) This expanded use is based on the general simple principle:

## *ANY BEHAVIOR CAN BE SEPARATED INTO SMALL, MANAGEABLE PARTS.*

When situational behaviors are broken down into their separate parts, all the parts must be put in the same order n which they are performed. While this is relatively easy to figure out for task behavior, it is more difficult when emotional, or relationship behaviors are involved. Fortunately, most parents and adults have the benefits of their own childhood experiences and maturity to aid them with this task. This issue also will be discussed in greater detail later in this text.

### Problematic Situation Behaviors

For the real case of Janine being used here as the example, the first challenge was to learn and examine her behaviors in the same depth as illustrated for the general, simple task of hand-washing that was discussed above.

Janine was a 7-year-old without friends at school or home. At school, following brief interactions with her peers on the playground, her behaviors always resulted in such conflict that no one would play with her. Furthermore, her behaviors, both on the playground and in the classroom, were often so disruptive that the activities of everyone around her were affected. Because these anti-social behaviors affected the development of her classmates, the public school administrators threatened to expel her from the public school system.

Although Janine had several sessions with both the school psychologist and a private practice psychologist, there was no sustainable improvement. When this case was referred to me, it was made very clear that my work with her would be the last chance for her to remain in the school system.

Janine's parents admitted, when I spoke with them on the telephone, that they didn't really know what their daughter was doing at school. So, I first visited the school to meet with her teacher in order to learn exactly what she was doing, i.e. to identify Point A. (In all dialog reproduced in the examples that follow, I refer to myself as "**Coach**".) The conversation at Janine's school was as follows:

> **Coach:** "I've been told Janine has a problem interacting with her peers, and it is serious enough that the State referred her to work with me. Can you help me understand the problem?"

> **Teacher:** "Yes, that's easy. I've watched her many times in the classroom, and on the playground during recesses and lunchtime. It's quite sad. No one can interact with her for very long, and she causes trouble with children who are playing nicely."

> **Coach:** "I understand that this has been going on for quite awhile, and now no one will have anything to do with her. What does she do in the situation where another child is all alone on the playground? How does she behave towards getting them to play?"

> **Teacher:** "Well, that's the way the disturbances have started. She's friendly in her initial approach and talk of playing something, like follow the leader on the monkey bars, etc. but she makes it clear that if they do, she will be the leader. If the other child challenges why she gets to be the leader, Janine says that, since she thought of it, she's the boss and the leader.

> This always leads to an argument and fight, with both of them getting angry. Then the child says they won't play with her and runs away with Janine standing there alone and furious.

> At that point, if the other child has joined into anything else, Janine will start trouble. For example, if they're shooting baskets, she'll grab the basketball and either run off with it, or throw it over the fence, or something that totally disrupts everyone else's playtime.

> Discipline hasn't worked, and psychological treatment has not been successful. So, at this point, the principal has warned her parents that she will be expelled from this school unless you can help her."

During this meeting, it was decided to first focus on the playground behaviors because they seriously affected her ability to make friends, and were more disruptive for everyone than her behaviors in the classroom. When we reviewed the teacher's report of Janine's actual playground behaviors, it was possible to identify important information about her problem behaviors from the conversation. To put this information into a practical format for use with this method of coaching for behavior change, parts of the conversation were re-written with the key parts of her actual behaviors shown as **bold** print in the following:

> She's **friendly in her initial approach and talk of playing** something, like follow the leader on the monkey bars, but she makes it clear that if they do, she will be the leader. If the other child challenges why she gets to be the leader, Janine says that, **they have to play what she wants**, so she gets to be the **boss and the leader.**
>
> This always leads to an **argument and fight**, with both of them getting angry. Then the child says they won't play with her and runs away with **Janine getting left** and standing there alone and furious.

Now with the above re-write of the conversation, it was very easy to identify and make a **list** of the following parts as **Janine's Actual Behaviors – List A**:

### Janine's Actual Behaviors – List A

1. She approaches a child in a friendly way
2. She talks about playing
3. She **talks and acts bossy**
4. She **dictates** the play
5. She **argues** to get her way
6. She gets left

In the above list, only the problem parts of each behavior step are shown in **bold** print. Converting all information to a format that can lead to such a simplified list is important in this method because, ultimately, it will be transferred to the behavior map as **Point A.** Only one other task must be done with List A in order to make it completely compatible with the Map format. It needs to be re-written in an inverse order, as shown below:

### Janine's Actual Behaviors – List A    (Inverse Order)

6. She gets left
5. She **argues** to get her way

4. She **dictates** the play

3. She **talks and acts bossy**

2. She talks about playing

1. She approaches a child in a friendly way

### Finding Janine's Point A

At this stage, finding Janine's Point A behavior on the map only requires answering two basic questions:

a.   On which side of the behavior map should the Actual Behaviors, **Point A,** be located, i.e. the personal, relationship or reality side?

b.   Once that side is identified, where, along that side, are the behaviors approximately located?

For the situation of Janine trying to make a playmate, her interactive behaviors towards her peers always had the same results, i.e. problems and failures. Thus, it was obvious that Janine's Actual Behaviors were along the Relationship side of her map.

Once the Relationship side was identified, it was only necessary to choose an approximate location along that side to show where her behaviors were actually located as **Point A.** In the Introduction, it was learned that the Relationship side consists of a range with the two extremes, **isolated** and **engulfed**. To determine which extreme Janine was nearest, one need only observe the effect of her behaviors on her peers. In her case, it always resulted in driving them away, or being isolated from them. Therefore, from that observation, it was logical to place Janine's **behaviors** nearest to the **isolated** end on the relationship side.

Janine's Point A behavior can now be **mapped**. This simply means to take each item from the separate behavior parts of Janine's **List A** and copy it onto the appropriate place on the map, so that *each separate part on the list is identical to one separate part on the map*. If they maintain the exact positions on the list and map, then Part 1 on the list is equal to Part 1 on the map, etc. Figure 1-1 shows the map with Janine's Point A located near the isolated endpoint.

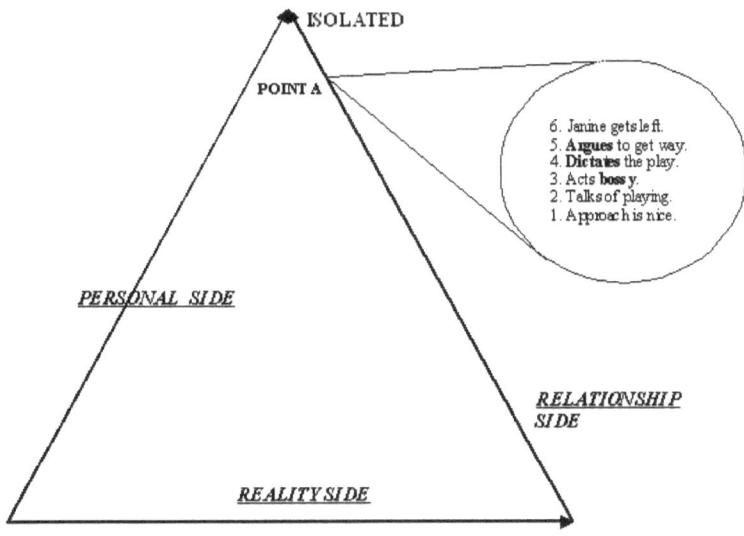

**Figure 1-1 Behavior Map showing Janine's Point A location, based on her List A of actual behaviors.**

Mapping is a highly important concept in this method for several reasons. Firstly, it gives coaches a visual aid for comparing problem behaviors with corrected behaviors for any situation. As such, it can be used as a quick way for tracking actual progress towards correcting the behaviors. Secondly, it provides a logical tool for **coaching the person to change** their behaviors to more closely match the appropriate and effective behaviors located at Point B. (The mapping concept for behaviors as first applied by the author as shown in Appendix A.)

## Identifying the Problem Behavior Side – In General

Janine's problematic behaviors on the school playground were used as the example for completing this step of the method. As previously emphasized, for locating a person's Point A behavior on the map, the coach only needs to know the side and approximate location along that side. To simplify this step, only the two most commonly used sides are discussed in this example for behavior placement - the personal and relationship sides. While reality issues may, at times be the primary presenting problems, in most cases they are more manifested in the personal, or relationship planes of the behaviors, and can be addressed more easily in those areas.

With Janine's problem, it was obvious that her behaviors belonged on the Relationship side. Since some situational behaviors may not be as clear as Janine's, parents and coaches need to have an easy way to determine placement on the map. To do that, the coach only has to answer the following general question about the person's behaviors:

> Is the primary *effect* of their actual behavior in the area of their relationships with others, in the area of their personal functioning, or in how they deal with reality?

The answer to this question <u>determines</u> the side of the map for locating the **Point A** behaviors. Limiting the choice to only one side isn't meant to imply that the effect of their problem in another area is unimportant. It simply means that the person's development is potentially more at risk in the area identified. Janine's problem is a good example. In some areas of her functioning, she was reported to be developmentally on track, especially in terms of her personal behaviors, i.e. thinking, feeling, acting and physiology. However, her social development was seriously off track because of her behaviors/interactions towards her peers.

**<u>Locating Point A – In General</u>**

After finding the correct side of the map to visually locate the problem, it is necessary to find the approximate location of the actual behaviors. In a similar way to how the correct side was found, coaches only have to choose from a list of choices that best complete the following statement.

For the person, the effect of using the problem behavior is:

| | | |
|---|---|---|
| a. | They are **ISOLATED** from others. | (Relationship extreme) |
| b. | They are **ENGULFED** by others. | (Relationship extreme) |
| c. | They are **IMPULSIVE** in their actions. | (Personal extreme) |
| d. | They are **INHIBITED** in their actions. | (Personal extreme |
| e. | They are **SELF-FOCUSED** in terms of reality. | (Reality extreme) |
| f. | They are **OTHERS-FOCUSED** in terms of reality. | (Reality extreme) |

Making a choice from the above list determines the proximity to the midpoint on which children with problem behaviors are found. It only needs to be approximate because the map is, primarily, only a visual aid for helping identify the person's behaviors as different compared to when they are near the midpoint.

When the school staff reviewed Janine's List A, the only logical selection was the first choice, or "a." For Janine, the primary effect of choosing the behaviors she was using was greater isolation from others. As a result, her **Point A** behaviors shown in Figure 1-1 were placed close to the extreme for the Relationship side, i.e. **isolated**. Indeed, Janine was socially isolated and would continue to be that way if her behaviors remained the same without correction. Janine's parents were not yet involved in this part of the process, however, they would be advised of these important results concerning her school behaviors and involved in all of the following steps of this method.

## Chapter 1 Checklist: Things to remember

- A person's actual behaviors in a situation can be broken down into small, separate parts and listed in the logical order they occur.
- The separate parts listed for a person's actual behaviors can be compared directly to the separate parts listed for the expected behavior in the same situation.
- Point A behaviors are **mapped** by writing the list of parts for the actual behaviors directly onto the map at the correct place.
- Correct placement of Point A is done by first finding the side, and then finding the approximate location along that side.
- The side is identified by the answer to a single question:

   *Is the primary <u>effect</u> of their actual behavior in the area of their relationships with others, in the area of their personal functioning, or in how they deal with reality?*

If the answer to this question is "relationships", then Point A is located somewhere along the Relationship side. If the answer is "personal functioning", then Point A is located somewhere along the Personal side of the map. If the answer is "reality," then Point A is located along the Reality side of the map.

- The approximate location of Point A along the side of the map is found by selecting from a list, the one choice that best completes the following statement:

For the person, **the effect of using the problem behavior is:**

a. They are **ISOLATED** from others.          (Independent Relationship Extreme)

b. They are **ENGULFED** by others.          (Dependent Relationship Extreme)

c. hey are **IMPULSIVE** in their actions.          (Unregulated Personal Extreme)

d. They are **INHIBITED** in their actions.          (Over-regulated Personal Extreme)

e. They are **SELF-FOCUSED** in terms of reality.          (Reality extreme)

f. They are **OTHERS-FOCUSED** in terms of reality.          (Reality extreme)

- Based on this selection, **Point A** is placed between the midpoint and the behavior extreme along that side. Keep in mind that achieving the operating behaviors located near the midpoint along any side is the **ultimate goal** with this method for coaching for change.

# Chapter 2

## *Step 2: What should they be doing?*

*When traveling to any new Point B, it is important to know what one must do to actually get there.*

Once the first step has been successfully completed so that there exists a **"List A"** for the actual behaviors, along with the location of **Point A** on the behavior map, then Step 2 can be addressed.

### Janine's Expected Behaviors

Following my meeting with the teacher and other staff at school, I met with Janine's parents. This was a very important meeting, because it was the beginning of the training that parents using this method needed to be able to coach effectively. For all of my cases, it was very important to train the parents to replace me as the coach once the child made sufficient behavior changes to be back on their developmental track. In the future, it would be up to them to assist Janine with maintaining the initial changes, and any additional changes in her behaviors.

After the normal introductory information, the conversation went like this:

**Coach:** "I met with Janine's teacher and other school staff and heard about her problems with her peers at school. I understand that some of it may also be going on here at home. Is that right?"

**Parent:** "Yes, that's right."

**Coach:** "Can you tell me how you see the problem?"

**Parent:** "She fights with everyone who she tries to play with and can't make any friends."

**Coach:** "Do you know exactly what she's doing in these situations?"

**Parent:** "No, not really. We're not out there with her."

**Coach:** "Well, I will talk to Janine to find out about that. Tell me, regardless of what she is actually doing, what do you think she should be doing to make friends or have a playmate?"

**Parent:** "Well, you know, being nice and getting along, not fighting and all with everyone she meets."

**Coach:** "Can you be a little more specific? Let's say she sees someone she'd like to play with standing alone on the playground. What do you think Janine should do in that particular situation?"

**Parent:** "Well, first she should go up to them in a friendly way. Then maybe a greeting and some talk about playing something. Janine should be nice, and talk and act friendly the whole time. After that, together they should decide what they want to play and go ahead with it. Oh, yeah, they should also take turns being the leader and normal stuff like that when they play."

**Coach:** "Do you think that would work for Janine for having a playmate and maybe make friends?"

**Parent:** "Yeah. I know that's what we did when we were her age and all along. That's the way they're supposed to act, isn't it?"

**Coach:** "It sounds right to me. What you just described is what I call the **Expected Behaviors**, and as you pointed out, these are the behaviors that everyone is supposed to use, more or less, in these kinds of situations. Now, all we have to do is examine exactly what Janine is doing and how it is different in that kind of situation, then compare it to what you just described."

The above dialogue was significant because it validates several important points upon which this method is based. First, it shows that Janine's parents knew, albeit unconsciously, the expected behaviors, that their daughter should have been using in the playtime situation. Her parents were no different than any of the other parents that I had met and worked with over many years. Most parents seem to basically know what behavior their children should be using in most situations. They may not be able to articulate it very well, but it is knowledge that most have. This is very important in this method for coaching and changing behaviors, because if the coach recognizes the most appropriate and effective behaviors to be used in different situations, then they can very easily understand and locate **Point B - the expected behaviors**, on the behavior map!

Second, as a therapist/coach, I had learned that the most effective way of working with behavior problems was to go to the places these problems actually occur - the real situations. When talking with parents about real situations, it became obvious to me that the expected ways of acting were just as apparent and meaningful to parents as to the professionals. Therefore, parents don't have to become, or even involve, professionals to help their children in most situations, because they already know what they need to know. In my opinion, most parents only need minimal training to be able to effectively coach them for making the correct changes in behavior! These factors and insights helped in developing this method that would be accessible and practical for anyone to use successfully.

### Creating Janine's Point B Behaviors List

Janine's parents were good models to illustrate how this works. We knew that Janine had problems in the relationship area and that her parents knew what she *should* have been doing. We will now recall the above conversation with her parents and highlight in **bold** print the key behaviors they mentioned when asked to be precise about what Janine should do in the situation of approaching another child all alone on the playground:

> "Well, she should go up to them in a **friendly** way. Then, maybe **a greeting and some talk about playing** something. Janine should **be nice, and talk and act friendly** the whole time. After that, **together they should decide** what they want to play and go ahead with it. Oh, yeah, they should also **take turns** being the leader and stuff like that when they play."

As with the Teacher in determining Point A, if this conversation is re-written in a slightly different format so that it resembles a list, it looks like the following:

> she should go up to them in a **friendly** way
> make a **greeting and some talk about playing**
> Janine should **be nice, and talk and act friendly**
> **together they should decide** what they want to play
> go ahead with it, (**play**)
> **take turns being the leader**, etc.

Since these parents also said that's what they would have done in that situation, they either called upon their own personal experiences, or their basic knowledge of childhood relationships. Taking the above information and putting it into a more concise form that can be viewed as corrections to Janine's separate actions, we had what they thought would work better for the playground situation. Therefore using the parent's feedback, it was possible to create **LIST B - Janine's Corrected Behaviors:**

## Janine's Corrected Behaviors - LIST B

1. She approaches a child in friendly way
2. She talks about playing
3. She **doesn't talk and act bossy**
4. They **both decide** what to play
5. **Without arguing**
6. Janine gets to play

Now, making the above list was easy because it was based upon precisely what the parents knew would be appropriate and effective behaviors. Without being aware of it, they already knew the behaviors expected - the Point B behaviors in the situation given here. Thus, when it was time to locate Janine's Point B on the Behavior Map, List B became Point B. Before adding this information, the list was edited slightly for brevity, and inverted as follows:

## Janine's Corrected Behaviors - LIST B    (Inverse order)

6. Janine gets to play
5. Janine does not **argue**
4. They **both decide** what to play
3. She **doesn't talk and act bossy**
2. She talks about playing
1. She approaches a child in friendly way

The Point B information was then added to the Janine's behavior map for this situation, and is shown in Figure 2-1 below, along with her actual behaviors at Point A.

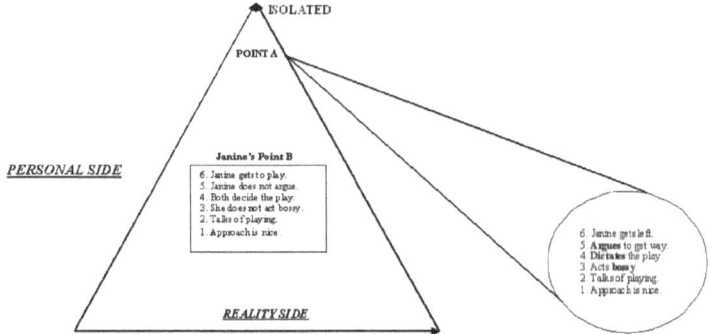

**Figure 2-1 Janine's behavior map showing Janine's Point A and the Point B behaviors for the playground situation.**

Listing the key parts of the expected behaviors for a situation on this map is important in this method, because once the problem behavior information is added, it allows for quick comparison. Since space is limited for writing the information on the form for Point B, a separate form is useful to work up the descriptive lines in a shorthand-type of way that will fit on the map. Because the staircase approach is important for showing the trials and changes of each part leading up to the Point B behaviors, it was necessary to relocate the Point A List of behaviors to the lower part of the map.

## Making the Lists

Making a list of actual and expected behaviors in this method doesn't require working with a professional for help as Janine's parents had to do. A simple "recipe" for doing this for a person of any age using this method is shown below:

A. Pick a typical situation where the person has a recurring problem.

B. Use one or two lines on a piece of paper to generally describe the situation, i.e. "The child approaches a peer on the playground to get them to play with her, etc."

C. Under the description, write the question:
   What is the person trying to do in this situation?

D. Write the answer to this question, i.e. "Janine is trying to find someone to play with, and make a friend."

E. Next, write the question:
   What is the person actually doing in this situation?

F. Beginning with the very first thing that was being done, **list each separate part in the logical order** they were done in the situation used.

G. Next, write the question:

What should the person be doing in this situation?

H. Beginning with the very first thing that <u>should be done</u>, list each separate part in   the logical order they would have to be done to be successful in the situation being addressed.

At completion, the paper will look like this form:

A **typical situation** where the person has a problem is _____

What the person is **trying to do** in this situation is _____

What behaviors is the person **actually using** in this situation?

1. (the 1st separate part)

2. (the 2nd separate part)

3. (etc., continue until all behavior parts have been listed.)

THIS IS THE LIST FOR ACTUAL BEHAVIORS (POINT A) ON THE BEHAVIOR MAP.

When corrected, the behavior parts the person **<u>should</u>** be using in this situation are:

1. (the 1st separate part)

2. (the 2nd separate part)

3. (etc., continue until all behavior parts have been listed.)

4. Add lines, as necessary!

THIS IS THE LIST FOR CORRECTED BEHAVIORS (POINT B) ON THE BEHAVIOR MAP.

The completed lists may then written at the appropriate locations on the map with the **Actual Behaviors List** as **Point A**, and the **Corrected Behaviors List** as **Point B**. While Point B is always in the same location, Point A must be uniquely determined for each situation.  As shown below, in

Figure 2-2, the location for writing the Point B List is always located in the center of the diagram.

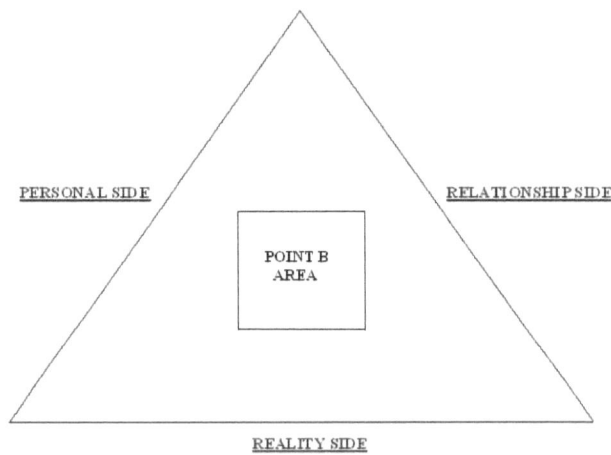

**Figure 2-2 General Behavior Map with the Point B area shown for adding the Point B List.**

## Chapter 2 Checklist: Things to Remember

- Parents **know** the expected behaviors, Point B, in most situations in their culture.
- The behaviors used in situations are **situational behaviors**.
- All situational behaviors have **content**.
- The content of situational behaviors can be **task, emotional, relationship**, or a combination of all three.
- Examining the situational behaviors is the starting point for changing children's, or any person's behaviors.
- Identifying the expected behaviors in any situation is based on the question:

  *What behaviors should the person be using in this situation?*

- Any situational behaviors can be broken into small, separate/ manageable parts.

- The separate parts of the expected behaviors in any situation must be listed in the logical order that they would normally occur. Don't skip any parts, and list as many as possible!

- The separate parts of the situation used can be written in the order listed on the behavior map in the space provided in the central area for Point B.

# Chapter 3

## *Step 3: Comparing Behavior Lists and Choices*

*During any travel, it is necessary to compare the intermediate locations with the map locations all along the way.*

Once the task of making the lists of Point A and Point B behaviors is completed, it is a relatively easy task to compare the two for deviations, and locate the logical starting point for matching them up. As discussed previously, this simply means matching each part separately until the two lists are equal, or nearly the same. For example, if numbered in the same logical order that they occur, then the #1 of the Point A list should match as closely as possible to the #1 of the Point B list, etc.

| Point A list | | Point B list |
|:---:|:---:|:---:|
| #1 | = | #1 |
| #2 | = | #2 |
| #3 | = | #3 |

etc.

When making this one-to-one comparison of parts, the parts that needed to be changed are those on the Point A list that are not close to being equal to the same numbered parts on the Point B list. The lists from Step 1 and Step 2 for Janine's situation will be repeated here as the example.

When Janine's two lists are lined up side-by-side so that each behavior part on **LIST A** can be directly compared with the same behavior part on **LIST B**, we have the following versions (abbreviated to save space):

| LIST A - Janine's Actual Behaviors | LIST B - Janine's Corrected Behaviors |
| --- | --- |
| 1. Approaches in friendly way | 1. Approaches in friendly way |
| 2. They talk about playing | 2. They talk about playing |
| 3. Janine **talks and acts bossy** | 3. Janine **doesn't talk and act bossy** |
| 4. Janine **dictates** what to play | 4. Both **decide** what to play |
| 5. Janine **argues** to get her way | 5. **Without arguing**, they play |
| 6. Janine gets left | 6. Both agree to play again |

At a glance, only the first two parts of Janine's actual playground behaviors on LIST A **match** those on LIST B. The parts on Janine's LIST A that needed to be changed to match the Point B list are shown in **bold** print.

Next, the list will be re-written in an inverted form, with the initial part at the bottom and the final part at the top. (The reason for inverting the order will become clear near the end of this section.)

| LIST A - Janine's Actual Behaviors | LIST B - Janine's Corrected Behaviors |
| --- | --- |
| 6. Janine gets left | 6. Both agree to play again |
| 5. Janine **argues** to get her way | 5. **Without arguing**, they play |
| 4. Janine **dictates** what to play | 4. Both **decide** what to play |
| 3. Janine **talks and acts bossy** | 3. Janine **doesn't talk and act bossy** |
| 2. They talk about playing | 2. They talk about playing |
| 1. Approaches in friendly way | 1. Approaches in friendly way |

By inspection, there are four parts on Janine's list of Actual Behaviors in the playground situation that do not match the same numbered parts on the Point B list. They are #3, 4, 5 and 6. Part #6 was not shown as **bold** for correction, because this was an anticipated outcome of the improved interaction and was expected to change only when the other parts were corrected successfully.

Once the lists were compared and the unmatched parts marked, the coaching process was ready to begin in Chapter 4, Step 4, to help the person make new choices in those parts of their behaviors in that situation. From my experience, children and other individuals *wanting to change* participate very well in this method. They are usually capable of seeing and finding solutions to many of their own problems once they see them broken into the small, separate parts that they can understand and manage.

Assuming Janine would agree to try something different to replace those parts not matching Point B, a new list could be made showing the new choices of behavior she was willing to try. These new choices would replace the problem parts on her Point A list. The new choices shown on the list below are written in ***bold italic*** print.

| POINT A BEHAVIORS | ***JANINE'S NEW CHOICES*** | POINT B BEHAVIORS |
|---|---|---|
| **5. Argues to get way** | ***5. Compromises*** | 5. Plays |
| **4. Dictates what to play** | ***4. Decides together*** | 4. Both decide |
| **3. Talks and acts bossy** | ***3. Will not act bossy*** | 3. Talk & act friendly |
| 2. Greet & talk of play | 2. Greet & talk of play | 2. Greet & talk of play |
| 1. Approach in friendly way | 1. Approach in friendly way | 1. Approach in friendly way |

After reviewing these lists there was a clear view of the changes Janine needed to make in order for her Point A list to match the Point B list in the playground situation. If she agreed to try the new choices, they would be direct replacements for the old ones that did not work well. If the coaching process for trying the new choices worked successfully with Janine, then, ultimately, her new Actual Behaviors List would closely match the Point B List.

Now, actually making the four changes listed here could be very hard for some children, especially individuals like Janine. It was very likely she would have to improve and prove herself one small part at a time. Therefore, it was unrealistic to expect Janine, or any child to immediately begin using the new behavior parts successfully and at all once.

Typically, such changes occur in a "**staircase**" fashion, where the first change is the first step on the staircase to change, the second change is the second step, etc. By the time they get to the very top of the staircase, all previous parts are in place and they are at the desired outcome for the corrected/expected behaviors. For Janine, the absolute top of her staircase of change was "**Makes a Friend.**" The staircase concept is used here as both a visual aid and to reflect the progression to ultimately be shown on the map. Figure 3-1, shown below is the staircase for change developed for Janine.

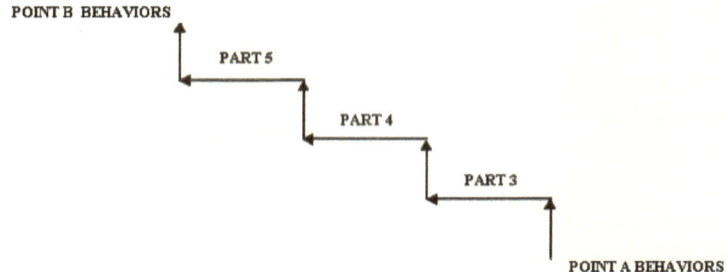

**Figure 3-1 Janine's Staircase for Change.**

The reason for writing the behavior parts in the inverted form should now be apparent. Transferring them onto the steps of a rising staircase symbolizes the personal growth taking place in the 5-STEP method. The staircase presentation is also a good visual tracking aid for both the coach and the person making the behavior changes.

The staircase of change also can be directly transferred to the behavior map to show the new choices of behaviors in the steps that they should occur, i.e. the first change/step for Janine to make is part #3, the second is part # 4, etc. Figure 3-2 shows her new choices as a staircase from Point A to Point B. In addition, a **Trial Data Block** and associated trial data entry points are shown on this map, and will be used in future activities with Janine.

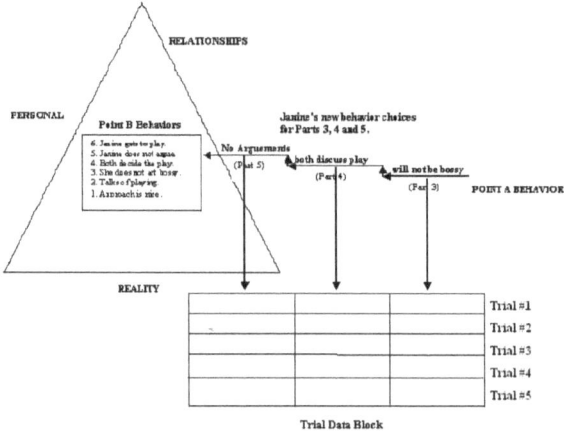

**Figure 3-2 Janine's Behavior Map with new choices for reaching Point B, and the Data Block for entering data from the Trials.**

## Chapter 3 Checklist: Things to remember

- The person making the changes must be involved in choosing the new behavior parts they will commit to try.

- Comparing the lists of Point A and Point B is done on a one-to-one basis, i.e. part #1 on the Point A list is compared to part #1 on the Point B list.

- The parts that match are those that are nearly equal. The parts that are not nearly equal are the parts that need replaced.

- The list of person's new choices must be based on the parts from their Point A list that need replaced.

- Replacing any number of parts is a process of change that looks like a staircase, with the first changed part being the first step in the staircase, etc. until all have been made.

- At the top of the staircase for change is the desired outcome, on the top of the Point B list.

- The staircase for change can be shown visually, and used on the behavior map as an aid to both the coach and person making the changes.

# Chapter 4

## Step 4: Preparing the Person For Behavior Change

*The importance of <u>preparation</u> for change from one place to another cannot be overestimated.*

### The First Meeting

Until now, the person with the behavior problems has not played an active role in the 5-STEP method. Steps 1, 2 and 3 focused on the coach's preparation and planning for effectively using this method. The time has finally come for talking with the individual and initiating the formal process of change. This step prepares them for leaving the known and comfortable, albeit dysfunctional, behaviors at Point A to attempt using the unfamiliar and unproven behaviors at Point B.

When working with children and young adults, coaches need to keep in mind how much anxiety young people can experience when they have to try <u>anything</u> new, or different, even if it is guaranteed to be better! This step initiates the whole process of change, and when done correctly, several significant developmental building blocks are put in place for the individual including:

- The capability to see their problem more realistically
- The motivation to attempt different choices
- Enhanced feelings of empowerment to begin the unknown process

- Enhanced commitment to the process of change

This is all accomplished by asking **five key questions** during conversation with the person. As designed, these questions are worded and arranged in a very specific way for use as a *script to be followed* as closely as possible. Also, for coaches/parents, or other trusted non-professional figures to be perceived and accepted as credible in the role for coaching for change, some other details are important for success, including meeting in the most effective setting and communicating the most effective behaviors towards the individual while using the script.

All these conditions will be given very clearly as guidelines whenever scripts are involved, as in the following.

### Step 4: The Optimum Coaching Setting

- Find a private, comfortable and informal place
- Coach and person making changes only, no siblings, peers, or other adults
- No distractions, i.e. interruptions by others, TV, telephone, etc.
- Satisfy the person's normal needs first, i.e. food, drink, etc.
- Schedule the session at a time when the person is most attentive, not tired nor distracted by thinking about other activities

### Step 4: The Coach's Behaviors

- Listen, listen, listen, and <u>really hear</u> what they are saying!
- Warm, caring, sincere and trustworthy attitude
- Informal, relaxed with controlled voice, i.e. warm, even, etc.
- Expressive eye contact, i.e. friendly, caring, etc.
- Factual and unemotional with information
- Non-blaming and non-judgmental responses

### Step 4: The Key Script Questions

1. *What happened in the situation?*
2. *What do you think went wrong?*
3. *What did you want to happen?*
4. *What could you have done differently?*

*5. Would you be willing to try some different choices?*
*6. May I help you with those choices?*

Regardless of the content, or usefulness of the answers to the first four questions, **a "yes," answer is mandatory for the last two questions** before any change of the problem behaviors are possible. Any other answers may indicate they are not ready for change, or something went wrong during this meeting. In any case, it must be emphasized that, if there are not "yes" answers, then this step must be repeated as often as necessary until there are "yes" answers to questions #5 and 6. See Chapter 7 about method variations and how to proceed when this situation occurs

When acting as the coach, some parents may have trouble with this step if they are unable to assume the proper behaviors towards their child due to past conflicts, attitudes or pessimistic feelings about their ability to change. For example, parents with a teen who often has been thrown out of school for inappropriate behaviors may not believe the child can ever change. In these kinds of situations, practicing this step by role-playing with another adult may help improve the detachment that is needed. If this fails, then the parents will not be able to act as the coach for the desired changes, and another person perceived as credible and trusted by the child will be necessary to act as the coach for change.

### Step 4 Example

Now, we can return to Janine's problem and apply this step to help her prepare for change. After the preliminary rapport-building conversation was completed, the key questions were asked. This was the conversation with the key questions shown in **bold** print:

**Coach:** Janine, I understand there has been a problem with you having playmates and making friends. When's the last time you tried here at school?
**Janine:** At recess a couple days ago on the playground.
**Coach:** Can you tell me **what happened in that situation?**
**Janine:** Well, I went up to Maria and asked her to play, and all she did was fight with me and run away.
**Coach:** Well, if that's all you really did, why did she fight with you and run away? Are you sure there wasn't a little more to it than that?
**Janine:** Well, maybe there was a little more. We fought over what we were going to play and who was going to be the leader on the monkey bars. I told her what I wanted to do, but she got mean to me.
**Coach:** Janine, **what do you think went wrong in that situation?**

**Janine:** I don't know, I was really trying to be nice and all until she got mad.

**Coach:** Do you think it could have had anything to do with you deciding what the game was going to be and who was the leader?

**Janine:** I don't know. Maybe.

**Coach:** Janine, **what did you want to happen** out there on the playground with Maria?

**Janine:** I just wanted to play with her.

**Coach:** Did you also want to make a friend you could play with a lot?

**Janine:** Yeah.

**Coach:** Well, to get someone to play, or to make a friend, **what could you have done differently?**

**Janine:** I don't know. Maybe let her help pick the game?

**Coach:** That might be one good idea, Janine. I have some ideas about other things that might work, too. **Would you be willing to try some different choices** if it helps you make friends, or have playmates?

**Janine:** Yeah, sure. But, I don't know what all to do.

**Coach:** Well, that's where I come in. **May I help you with those choices?**

**Janine:** Sure, but Maria will probably never talk to me again.

**Coach:** Maybe you're right. But, don't be so sure. I have a feeling that if she knows you're acting differently, she'll might give you another chance. Would you like that?

**Janine:** Sure!

Notice that in the above example, there was absolutely <u>no</u> deviation from the script of questions and the order of their use with Janine. It is also important to point out at this stage that, by scrupulously following this script, *anyone can effectively coach another person* to achieve successful change.

At this point, the important preparatory blocks were in place for her to begin formal step-by-step change, i.e.

1.  *She was motivated* to do something different to get what she wanted.

2.  *She was empowered* to make different choices that would work better than what she had been doing.

3.  Finally, *she was committed* to trying the different choices, and working with someone who could help.

In short, the stage was set for Janine to actually begin trying out some of the new behavior parts!

## After the Commitment

Once the commitment has been made to work with a coach to make changes in behaviors, the meeting in Step 4 is continued to get the person's thoughts about new choices. The goal is to have them choose the same behavior parts as are on the list of expected behaviors at Point B. Therefore, they are to be encouraged to identify by themselves, the best available options for the situation. If they can do this, then **they <u>own</u> the ideas**, and are more likely to be successful in using them. Additionally, they begin to learn what it means to take responsibility for their choices, and develop a more realistic understanding of cause and effect. The payoff for this important addition can affect their position on the Reality Side of their Behavior map.

Since this method hinges on building the person's feelings of success one small step at a time along the way, it is important that they be guided, or "cued" at critical junctures to choose the ones most likely to succeed. For this reason, the *coach must assist them* to identify the best choices available in each of these situations.

During my coaching session with Janine, it was necessary to cue her to see/understand that one different choice on the playground was to let Maria help decide what to play. Continuing the conversation allowed her to see some of the options available in other parts.

**Coach:** Before talking more about how to decide the game, why don't we start at the beginning and see what else you could try with Maria, okay?

**Janine:** Well, okay.

**Coach:** How about the way you first went up to her, did you act friendly and greet her in a nice way?

**Janine:** Sure, I was really nice to her.

**Coach:** After that you talked about playing, right? How did that go?

**Janine:** Okay, I guess, but she said I was still **being bossy**.

**Coach:** Do you think you acted bossy to her?

**Janine:** I don't know. Maybe a little.

**Coach:** Well, if you were, I'll bet that'd be something easy for you to do differently if you try. What would you be willing to try doing the next time?

**Janine:** Not be bossy. Maybe let her talk more and pick other things to do?

**Coach:** Okay, that's good. How about **deciding what to play**, how did you two do that?

**Janine:** I told her I just wanted to play on the monkey bars, that's all. Oh, and that I'd be the leader.

**Coach:** Do you think it was okay with her that you decided without asking what she wanted to do first?

**Janine:** No, I guess not.

**Coach:** Is that something else you'd be willing to try differently?

**Janine:** Uh huh. Yeah.

**Coach:** How would you do that?

**Janine:** I'd just say, "Maria, I'd like to play follow the leader on the monkey bars, what would you like to do?"

**Coach:** That's very good, Janine. My guess is that'll work.

Going back to the last time you tried to play together, what happened after you told her what to play?

**Janine:** She said she didn't want to play that, and why was I always the leader? She got real mean to me!

**Coach:** How did she get mean? What did she do?

**Janine:** She argued with me, and said she didn't want to play. Then she ran away and started playing with some other kids.

**Coach:** Do you think the fight had anything to do with you insisting on what the game would be and that you would be the leader?

**Janine:** Well, maybe. But it <u>was</u> my idea, and I never get to be the leader. Everyone always tells me what to do at home and everywhere!

**Coach:** Okay, that's important and something that we can work on later, if you like. But for now, if you want to have someone to play with and make a friend, **would you be willing to not argue** about what to play?

**Janine:** I suppose. But they have to be fair, too!

**Coach:** Sure they do, and it's okay to tell them if they aren't. How about always having to be the leader? Would you be **willing to take turns** being the leader when you play, if it meant making a friend?

**Janine:** Yes.

With Janine's agreement to try some different choices in those parts not matching Point B, the list made in Step 3 was applicable. In our conversation, the new choices were shown in boldface print. The Step 3 list is repeated here for convenience.

| POINT A BEHAVIORS | *JANINE'S NEW CHOICES* | POINT B BEHAVIORS |
|---|---|---|
| 6. They play | 6. They Play | 6. They Play |
| **5. Argues to get way** | ***5. Janine does not argue*** | 5. No arguments |
| **4. Dictates what to play** | ***4. Both decide*** | 4. Both decide |
| **3. Acts bossy** | ***3. Will not act bossy*** | 3. Does not act bossy |
| 2. Greet & talk of play | 2. Greet & talk of play | 2. Greet & talk of play |
| 1. Approach in friendly way | 1. Approach in friendly way | 1. Approach in friendly way |

Janine was prepared and committed to working on changing her behaviors. Also, the behavior parts needing to be changed were identified and put in the order in which the changes would be made. The next step, Step 5 in Chapter 5, will focus on helping Janine make these changes.

## Chapter 4 Checklist: Things to remember

- The person making the changes **must be involved** in choosing the new behavior parts they will try
- The coach must help the person changing behaviors to identify the best new choices available
- Important 5-STEP foundation blocks are put in place for the person changing behaviors by the coach's listening ability, attentiveness and use of the following script of key questions:
    1. What happened in the situation?
    2. What do you think went wrong?
    3. What did you want to happen?
    4. What could you have done differently?
    5. Would you be willing to try some different choices?
    6. May I help you with those choices?
- A "yes," answer is mandatory for the last two questions before proceeding to Step 5
- More information about the importance in using scripts is found in Appendix A

# Chapter 5

## *Step 5: Traveling from Point A to Point B*

*To maintain the correct course of change, especially behavior, reliable <u>feedback</u> must be acquired all along the way.*

### <u>The Process</u>

The meeting with Janine in Chapter 4 prepared her, and set the stage for her to begin making behavior changes using new choices. With the proper coaching, she agreed that different choices were necessary, and was both empowered and motivated to use some of them on a trial basis. Regardless of outcome, after the first attempt at using a new choice, information would was available to be used as feedback to her about how well the trial went, in order to "correct her course of travel."

The sources of such feedback are from the same areas in which all behaviors are found, i.e. in terms of the triangle/pyramid, these are the **Personal, Relationships** and **Reality** areas. Some feedback information is external and verbal, and some is intuitive and unconscious. Despite the different types, it is essential that the same honest, <u>quality</u> feedback is perceived from each source in order to facilitate making effective changes. (Details about the Feedback Process are also found in Appendix A.)

A person's ways of dealing with feedback about their behaviors depends on their perception of the quality from each source.

A. Feedback from the **Personal** (internal) source is received as:
How the <u>person views</u> their own behavior.

B.  Feedback from the **Relationship** source is received as:
How the <u>person believes others view</u> their behavior.

C.  Feedback from the **Reality** source is received as:

How the <u>person views the outcome</u> of their behavior in the outside world.

After behavior trials are over and all of the feedback is available, persons making behavior changes begin to process the information in a very special way. Essentially, their **self-appraisal** serves as a sort of "performance review!" This self-appraisal is made on an unconscious level, but can have a very significant effect on their self-perceptions of how they feel about themselves, based on their actions in the given situation. More importantly, this mechanism of reviewing the feedback is important because, in large part, it determines whether they will continue using the new behavior, or abandon it forever!

The appraisal is based on information received from each source in the same way as regular feedback, except that it focuses on *how they did* when using the new behaviors. For this method of coaching, this basic appraisal approach can be analyzed and applied in the form of specific universal appraisal questions that can be used with everyone being coached.

**The Key Universal Appraisal Questions**
In this form, individuals are asking and receiving answers to the following self-appraisal questions when learning new behaviors:

*   Personal Feedback Source:
    **Based on <u>my</u> own view, "how did I do?"**
*   Relationship Feedback Source.
    **Based on the view of <u>others</u>, "how did I do?"**
*   Reality Feedback Source:
    **Based on my view of the <u>outcome</u> of my behaviors in the world, "how did I do?"**

When the answers/feedback to the above questions are, essentially: **"You did well, etc,"** <u>the person experiences and internalizes</u> the positive feelings and self-worth about themselves, and the sense of success needed to motivate them to continue using the new behaviors. Under these circumstances, the feedback from these 3 sources would be as shown in the following for Figure 5-1:

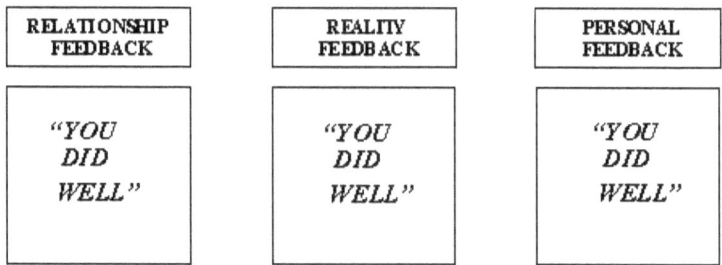

**Figure 5-1 Ideal feedback from the 3 different sources.**

### When the Process is Defective

Most people develop adequate abilities for dealing with external feedback, and their self-appraisal feedback without outside help, i.e. parents, etc. However, often this is not the case for children, or persons with problem behaviors. These individuals have developed a defective way, or system for handling feedback about their behaviors and reviewing their performance. It is defective because they either disregard, or alter/deny the feedback from some sources, i.e. others, reality.

The reasons for their dealing with it in this way are due to natural defense mechanisms that they have developed for avoiding the painful feelings that often come from honest feedback about their behavior deviations. In other words, if the truth hurts too much, the person's ego must defend and/or deny! In the interest of protecting their self-worth, ignoring or filtering the feedback is common, and totally understandable. Consequently, children, or other persons with problem behaviors can not be simply <u>pointed</u> in the right direction for success and then left alone to experience and appraise a new behavior. Using their defective feedback and self-appraisal system would only sabotage any trials, and guarantee failure. More importantly, perceiving early defeat, due to their faulty appraisal mechanism, may forever close the door for future trials using the improved choices of behavior.

Since the successful handling of feedback and self-appraisal are at the crux of this important step in changing behaviors, use of the faulty/defective system has to be interrupted. To do this, parents, or other adults acting as a coach *must temporarily intervene* in this area until sufficient change has taken place that the individual can successfully implement their own non-biased feedback process for themselves. This means that the person's feedback process first must be "managed" to produce the most effective results. Overriding the feedback and self-appraisal system at this stage only means presenting the most effective external information at the right time and in the right ways so that the natural defensive mechanisms can not interfere to sabotage the corrective behavior process. The person acting as the coach can do this very easily by scrupulously *following a specially designed "script" that feeds back the information as a specially designed package.*

### The Feedback Package

Because people with problem behaviors often have a defective system for dealing with feedback, it needs to be taken over and done for them until they are well on their way from Point A to Point B. Feedback given to these persons in the midst of making behavioral changes must perceive a positive "spin," or slant if it is to reinforce their continued use of new/trial behaviors. In other words, they need to hear, **"You did well,"** as much as possible when making such changes. Therefore, the feedback is orchestrated to give back the most effective information about the general features of their behavior.

The order for presenting these features is shown below.

- 1st Priority Feature - The result of their using the behaviors, i.e.
  *How well the behaviors worked.*

- 2nd Priority Feature - Their skill in using the behaviors, i.e.
  *How well the behaviors were performed.*

- 3rd Priority Feature - Their effort in using the behaviors, i.e.
  *How much effort they made.*

Giving feedback for the person's self-appraisal system, that uses these general features as if coming from each source, is made with a script presented in ways proven to motivate the person to continue using the new behaviors.

The script below is an example of the feedback given by a coach to a person who just completed the first trial of new behaviors for change from Point A towards Point B. The script is meant to be followed in the exact order given, and for best results, it should be worded as closely as possible to the way it is presented here:

1st Feedback Statement (From the Relationship source)

*"As I saw it, (person's name), you did well. I'm proud of you and the (result and/or skill and/or effort) of your new choice."*

2nd Feedback Statement (From the Reality source)

*"(Person's name), your new choice made a difference in how things turned out."*

3rd Feedback Statement (From the Personal Source)

*"(Person's name), you should really feel good about yourself for the way that worked out."*

It is important to be realistic when commenting about behavior features in the first feedback statement, because the person **knows** when the result has been bad, or their skills poor. Thus, as is often the case, the person's effort expended may be the only feature realistically applicable for positive feedback. Regardless of how first trials really turn out, it is very important that the person hears, "**You did well**," from each source of feedback even if it is only about the effort that they made!

Presented in the exact order and similar wording, this *package of feedback temporarily replaces their own faulty self-appraisal system.* After perceiving, "**You did well,**" from each of these sources, if believed credible, the person unconsciously sums up all three ideal feedback statements together to arrive at a total self-appraisal sum equal to, "**I did well!**" A complete diagram depicting this important process is shown below in Figure 5-2.

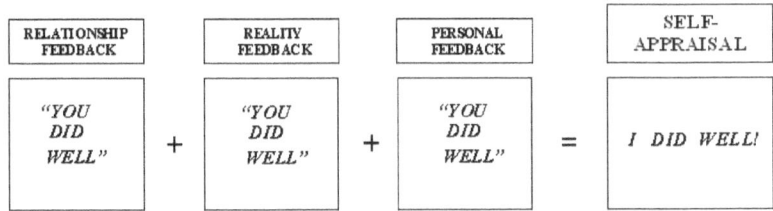

**Figure 5-2  The feedback summation process from the 3 sources involved in self-appraisal.**

While the first attempt at new behaviors, in fact, may not have been very good, the significance of the fact that they **risked** trying it to begin with, cannot be overestimated and must be celebrated somewhat. When someone with serious behavior problems experience <u>any</u> level of accomplishment with new choices, they usually can be motivated easily to continue using the new behaviors, if the appropriate supportive feedback is provided at the right time.

## Guidelines for Success

Complete Step 5 guidelines can now be written for giving the right feedback following trials of any new behaviors.

**Optimum timing** for giving feedback.

- As soon as practical after a behavior trial has been completed

**Optimum setting** for giving feedback.

- A private, comfortable and informal place
- The individual only. No family members, friends/peers or others present
- No distractions, i.e. interruptions, TV, telephone calls, etc.

**Optimum behavior** for coaches and parents giving feedback.

- _Listen_ by being 100% present during the conversations. This is a special level of attention to listen and really hear what is being said.
- Warm caring, sincere and positive. No negatives or criticism
- Informal, relaxed. Controlled voice, (friendly, warm, steady, etc.)
- Expressive eye contact, i.e. open, friendly, caring
- Reflect the person's positive feelings. Be optimistic about setbacks
- Capitalize on negative experiences as "learning" opportunities

## Basic Step 5 Feedback Script

Now that the essentials of Step 5 have been covered, we can now present the recommended basic script to be used by coaches when giving feedback.

1. **(Person's name), you did well. I'm proud of you and the**
   a.  result and/or
   b.  skill and/or
   c.  effort of your new choices.

2. **(Person's name), your new choice really made a difference in how things** turned out.

3a. (Person's name), you should feel really good about yourself for the way things turned out.

(or, alternative b)

3b. (Person's name), I bet you feel good about yourself for the way things turned out.

Assuming things went well during a trial, the unconscious response to the total feedback would be, "I <u>do</u> feel good about myself!" After several similar trials and responses, the personal source of their self-appraisal system will be working well enough for the individual to begin using that part on their own without the need for intervention, or external prompts from the coach. It is important to point out here that, <u>*under no circumstances*</u> should critical, or negative feedback ever be given at this stage. In fact, when using this method, critical, or negative feedback is never appropriate - regardless of the actual trial outcome.

## Continuing with Janine

A practical example of using Step 5 will be continuing the activity with Janine.

In Step 4, she committed and was prepared to try a new choice of behaviors. The first new choice for her to try was the first part of her behavior in the playground situation that did not match up with Point B. That was Part 3, her bossiness. With coaching, she agreed to try allowing the other children to suggest what to play.

Her first trial behaviors were to be attempted the next time she saw someone alone who she could play with during recess. As it turned out, the next day she saw Maria and took the risk of approaching her once again. As Janine had committed with the coach, she asked Maria to play without first declaring what she wanted to do. Maria was apprehensive about the idea of doing anything with Janine and didn't immediately respond. While still thinking about what to do, the bell rang and they had to return to class.

Though not a total trial success, it was a fair beginning because Janine did attempt a new behavior, and Maria didn't run away from her! As soon as we could talk later that same day, the basic Step 5 script was used with only minor variations with word order, etc.

**Coach:** I heard from your teacher that you were on the playground with Maria for awhile this morning. How did it go?

**Janine:** Not so good, we never got to do anything 'cause the bell rang!

**Coach:** Oh. Well, before the bell rang, what was going on?

**Janine:** We were talking about playing, and I didn't say what we had to play. So, she was thinking about it when we had to go in.

**Coach: You did well, Janine. I'm proud of you and the effort you made choosing not to be bossy.**

**Janine:** Yeah, but we didn't get to play anything, yet. She was only thinking about it.

**Coach:** That's only because the bell rang first. The way I see it, **Janine, your new choice already made a difference in how things turned out**, because Maria didn't run away. Isn't that true?

**Janine:** Oh, yeah that's right!

**Coach:** Janine, **you should feel really good about yourself for the way things turned out,** so far.

**Janine:** Yeah, but next time 1 hope we get to do something.

**Coach:** When can you try again?

**Janine:** Tomorrow morning.

The next day, Janine tried again. Maria picked shooting baskets and Janine didn't argue with her choice. They actually got to play together for a few minutes before being interrupted by others who wanted to play a real game. I saw Janine later that same day and continued Step 5.

**Coach:** I heard that you played with Maria for awhile today. How did it happen?

**Janine:** Well, 1 saw her alone again and just went up and said, "Do you want to play something?" And she said, "I don't know. Maybe." So, I said, "Okay."

**Coach:** Good. What did you play, and who decided?

**Janine:** Maria decided and I didn't fuss about it. We shot some baskets until a bunch of boys came and wanted to play a real game on the whole court.

**Coach:** That's really great. You finally got to play with Maria! From the way it sounds, **Janine, you did very well. I'm proud of you and your new choice to not be bossy.**

**Janine:** Yeah, but it was really hard. I don't like shooting baskets.

**Coach:** Well, one step at a time, Janine. Remember you really want someone to play with all the time and be a friend. So far, Janine, **your different choice already changed the way things turned out**, didn't it?

**Janine:** Yeah, it did.

**Coach:** The next time you try playing with Maria, would you be willing to add the other new choice we talked about, where you **discuss** what to play. That way you both decide without either of you being bossed.

**Janine:** Okay, maybe we'll get to play on the monkey bars. That's what I like best!

**Coach:** Great, Janine. **I bet you feel good about yourself for the way things have turned out** so far.

**Janine:** Yeah.

The above conversation used the basic script with minor variations only with the wording to make it sound natural. However, the basic wording of the feedback statements and the <u>order</u> of giving the messages is important. Therefore, to insure success with this method of coaching, especially in this part of Step 5, variations are not recommended.

It should be noted that Janine's lack of enthusiasm for responding to feedback script statements 3a and 3b was perfectly normal. At this stage, because they still have low self-esteem, it is rare for these children to admit, "Yes, I do feel good about myself!" In any case, whether expressed or not, *they will experience the good feelings* that accompany the successful results of behavior changes. Thus, on an unconscious level, their self-esteem will be elevated, and they will be well on their way to a corrected path for further change.

Now that Janine actually had actually begun her journey from Point A to B, the behavior map presented in Figure 3-2 showing her new choices could be used to track her progress, as shown below as Figure 5-3.

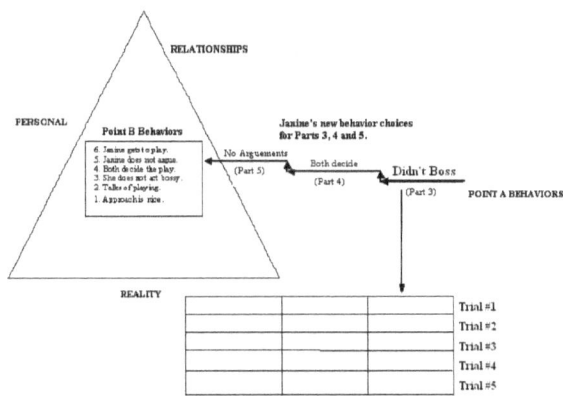

**Figure 5-3 Janine's Behavior Map for Step 5 showing the change in Part 3.**

In Figure 5-3, Part #3 of Janine's new choices was shown highlighted in **bold print** and changed to read, **"Didn't Boss,"** because she had already experienced two successful trials and self-appraisals for changing those parts of her problem behaviors. Using the Trial Date Block located at the bottom of the map, the two successful/positive points were then entered as "**+**" signs, shown below in Figure 5-4. Other useful code information that may be important to add for each trial will be discussed in the next chapter.

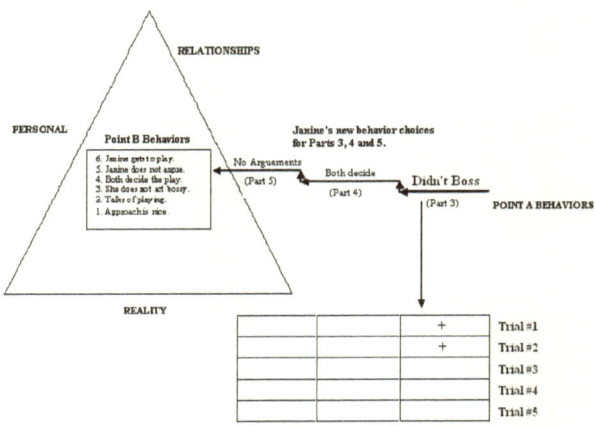

**Figure 5-4 Janine's two successful Trials for Part 3 Behaviors.**

Although additional practice still would be needed in this area, Janine's new behavior for Part #3 was moving in the right direction for achieving the behavior goal at Point B. Thus, Janine successfully began the process of moving up/progressing up one important step on her staircase for change required for taking her from Point A to Point B.

To complete Janine's program of improvement, I continued to meet with her in the role of a coach and use **Step 5** after each trial for Parts 4 and 5. Before all the remaining trials were completed, her behavior had improved so much that Maria had become the playmate and friend that Janine had wanted from the beginning. This was the strongest motivation of all for her continued use of the Point B behavior parts.

Finally when all of her behavior parts totally matched the Point B parts, *Janine no longer had a Point A.* Her new interactions with Maria, and other peers on the playground and in her neighborhood were all at Point B. She slowly began to be accepted by the other children and enjoyed the friendship of several. Helping Janine change behaviors took place in less than a month using this method, and meeting with her for about twice a week.

Janine's behavior map, given in Figure 5-4, illustrates how a person's progress can be tracked on a step-by-step basis while making changes. As shown in this figure, the map also can be used to keep track of the exact feedback used, and trial results for each step. This was achieved by using the **trial data block** shown at the bottom of the map. For Janine's example, only the + signs were shown. However, in reality, and as will be shown in the complete example provided in Chapter 9 of this book, all of the data will be entered with the short coded information given below:

+  means there was a positive trial

-  means there was a negative trial

IA means feedback statement #1A was used

IB means feedback statement #1B was used

2 means feedback statement #2 was used

3A means feedback statement #3A was used

3B means feedback statement #3B was used

A complete General Behavior Map with a data block provided for both the Personal Side and the Relationship side is shown below as Figure 5-5.

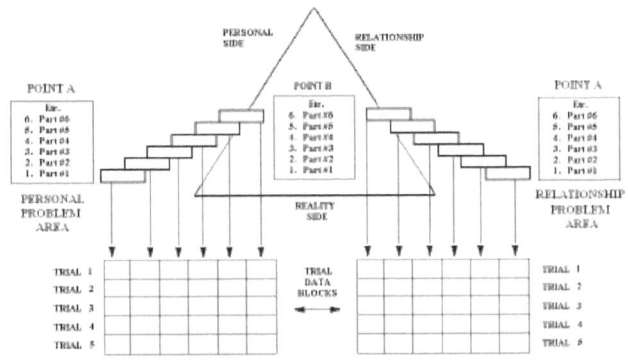

**Figure 5-5 Complete General Behavior Map**

## Chapter 5 Checklist: Things to Remember

- Information available to anyone about behavior is Feedback. In order to give it properly using this method, the coach must be capable of a special level of Listening – meaning to give 100% of focused attention to the person to really hear what they are saying, and to *manage the feedback* as a total package

- Feedback comes from the same places their behaviors are found, i.e. **Personal, Relationship,** and **Reality Feedback**

- When new behaviors have been tried, children use the feedback for an unconscious personal performance review, or **self -appraisal**

- The self-appraisal is based on the question, *"How did I do?"* Ideally, the answer is always, *"You did well."*

- Individuals with problem behaviors often have a defective way of handling feedback and their self-appraisal

- When individuals with problems are making changes, the coach must temporarily take over their feedback and self-appraisal system, by presenting it as a complete package using a script proven to be effective. After the basic guidance role for the coach, this is the most important function to be addressed and adhered to.

- The feedback package is made up of three scripted statements focusing only on the positive features of behavior trials as seen from each source, i.e. relationship, reality and personal.

- The general behavior features required, in order of their priority are:

    *a. Result - How well the behavior <u>worked</u>*

    *b. Skill -   How well the behavior was <u>performed</u>*

    *c. Effort -  How much <u>effort</u> they made*

- The order for delivering the feedback and the exact wording are very important and should not vary when giving these feedback statements:

### First Feedback Statement

**1. As I saw it, (Person's name), you did well.  I'm proud of you and the**

        **a. result and/or**
        **b. skill and/or**
        **c. effort**
            **of your new choice.**

### Second Feedback Statement

3.   (Person's name), your new choice really made a difference in how things  turned out.

## Third Feedback Statement

3a  (Person's name), you should really feel good about yourself for the way it worked out.

(or, alternatively,)

3b.   (Person's name), I bet you feel good about yourself for the way things  turned out.

- The behavior map can be used to keep track of trials and feedback.

# Chapter 6

## *Summary of the Method: Putting it all Together*

At this stage, it is important to point out that, although the examples used in this text are for parents coaching their own children having problem behaviors, the *applications for coaching using this method are not limited to any specific population.*   Anyone wanting, or needing assistance in changing their behaviors is appropriate and can benefit from the methodology presented here. For that reason, the Appendix is provided to document some the historical background of the coaching method as it was applied during a major State of Arizona Department of Juvenile Corrections **Substance Abuse Treatment Program** for adolescents in the early 1990's.  Additionally, during the same time period, this author had the opportunity to successfully work with adults with chemically dependent behaviors in different settings using the same general approach.

### The Big Picture Summary

Since details of the 5 step method of coaching for changing a person's behaviors have been presented in separate chapters, an overview and detailed summary of how to use the method will be useful before focusing on the complete example in the next chapter.

First, the "big picture" view is given to briefly present the process in the most concise way possible:

A.  Individuals needing and __*wanting*__ to change behaviors often require a coach for guidance, support and reinforcement during the stressful period of new/alternative behavior trials.

B.  For any social situation, the 5-step method of *Coaching for Behavior Change* teaches the coach to observe, analyze and separate **actual/** problematic behaviors into small, distinct parts that can be written on a list in the exact order used. This list of actual behavior parts is referred to as LIST A.

C.  The appropriate and effective behaviors *expected* in the situation can similarly be separated into the same number of small, distinct parts and written on a list in the same order as for List A. This list of expected behavior parts is referred to as LIST B. The parts on this list are the *goal behaviors* that are expected to be used by everyone in their culture.

D.  When the same individual parts on the two lists are directly compared, the parts on LIST A that do not closely match the same parts on LIST B are identified as the person's *deviant behaviors* that must change, or be corrected.

E.  The parts from the two lists then can be located on a unique 3-sided Behavior Map, where LIST A is POINT A, and LIST B is POINT B.

F.  The goal behaviors of POINT B are always found near the center of the map. The deviant behaviors of POINT A are located by asking specific *assessment questions*. These questions focus on the practical effects of the behaviors in the 3 areas of the person's functioning, i.e. personal, relationship, and reality. The answers to the questions determine the side of the triangular figure on which to locate Point A.

G.  Changing each deviant part on List A to become the same as the equivalent part on List B requires a series of behavior trials consisting of multiple attempts using new behavior choices with optimum feedback from the coach following each attempt.

H.  During the early stages of behavior trials, the **feedback is scripted** to provide the *optimum feedback package* needed for reinforcement of the person's self-esteem, and motivation/commitment to change at this stage.

I.  The combination of successful trials and optimum feedback for a minimum of 5 repetitions is typically sufficient to sustain the desired behavior changes for each part. More repetitions would be advantageous for improved competency and self-confidence.

## The Detailed Summary

Now that the overview has been presented, a more comprehensive summary of each of the **5** Steps, and the total process will be discussed to elaborate on important details.

## Step 1: What are they doing?

a. Choose a typical social situation where the problem behaviors are used.

b. Write down the actual behaviors observed, and separate them into small, individual actions/parts in exactly the same sequence they are used. Identify this list as **LIST A.**

c. For the selected situation, identify the side of the behavior map the actual behaviors will be located, based on the following assessment question:

Are the *effects* of the behaviors mainly in their **Relationships** with others, or mainly in their **Personal** functioning, or mainly in terms of how they deal with **Reality**?

- For the answer, "Relationships," the actual behaviors will be on the relationship side of the map as Point A. The approximate location on this side will be found by assessing the effect of the behaviors as being closest to one of the two endpoints identified as "Isolated" or "Engulfed."

- For the answer, "Personal functioning," the actual behaviors will be on the personal side of the map as Point A. The approximate location on this side will be found by assessing the effect of the behaviors as being closest to one of the two endpoints identified as "Impulsive" or "Inhibited."

- For the answer, "Reality," the actual behaviors will be on the reality side of the map as Point A. The approximate location on this side will be found by assessing the effect of the behaviors as being closest to one of the two endpoints identified as "Others-focused" or "Self-focused."

d. Take each of the parts documented in **List A** and, starting at the bottom of the map data block, write those same parts on the map side at the Point A location.

When writing these parts in the Point A block, Part 1 will be the 1ˢᵗ part listed and is to be placed in the block at the **lowest** position on the map, Part

2 will be the 2nd part listed and is to be placed in the nest position directly above Part 1, etc. The final part from the list should be at the highest position, at the top of the Point A block. See Figure 6-1, below, where a trial block has been placed on both the Relationship and the Personal sides. Notice the staircase effect for the parts of List A leading up to the top of List B.

### Step 2: What should they be doing?

a. For the situation selected, prepare a new list in the same order as for List A. Write all of the same number of small, individual parts making up the behaviors that would be **expected** in that situation. Identify this list as LIST B. This list will contain all of the important "corrected" parts that will become the behavior goals for change.

b. Take each of the parts documented in List B and, starting at the bottom of the map data block, write those same parts on the map side at the Point B location. When writing these parts in the Point B block, Part 1 will be the 1st part listed and is to be placed in the block at the **lowest** position on the map, Part 2 will be the 2nd part listed and is to be placed in the nest position directly above Part 1, etc. The final part from the list should be at the highest position, at the top of the Point B block.

Figure 5-6 shows the Point B block and parts locations along with the Point A parts.

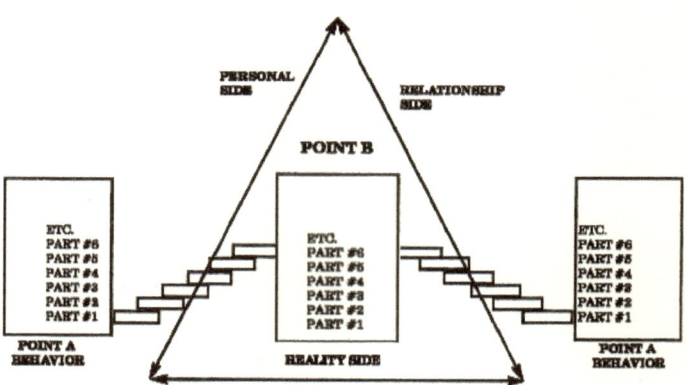

**Figure 6-1 General Behavior Map showing the staircase of parts for the Point A and Point B behavior lists.**

### Step 3: Comparing Behavior Lists and Choices

    a. Compare the list of behaviors for the chosen situation, as follows:

1. When both lists contain the same number of parts in the same locations, they can be lined up with each other to directly compare the behavior parts on the Point A list with the same behavior parts on the Point B list.

2. When compared, the parts on Point A *not closely matching* with those on Point B are the parts that require changing in order for the person's behaviors to be successful in the situation. In terms of our Behavior Map, making the changes necessary for Point A to match Point B in all parts, means the same as traveling from Point A to Point B on the map.

    b. **Select the Point B parts that are not matched as new behavior choices** and write them in the blank spaces for the Point A parts that are being replaced.

1. The new choices are based completely on the parts listed at Point B. For example, the new choices suggested to the person having the map shown below in Figure 6-2 are parts #4, 5 and 6 on the Point B list for the situation.

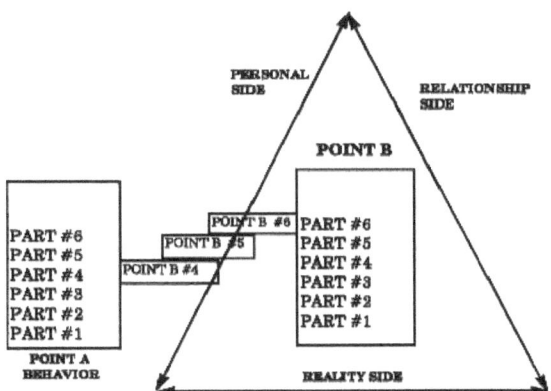

**Figure 6-2 Behavior Map example for person needing changes in Parts #4, 5 and 6 in order to travel from Point A to Point B on the Personal Side.**

### Step 4: Preparing the Person for Change

    a. Meet with the person in the following setting conditions:

1. Private, informal, comfortable, quiet

2. Only the coach and person making changes

3. No interruptions or distractions

4. Satisfy the person's normal needs first, i.e. food, drink, etc.

5. Schedule the session at a time when the person is most attentive not tired nor distracted by thinking about other activities

b. Required coach's behaviors during the meeting:

1. **LISTEN**, and be 100% present in order to really "hear" what they say

2. Caring, sincere, supportive and seen as trustworthy

3. Expressive eye contact, i.e. friendly, caring, etc.

4. Relaxed and informal with voice and body language

5. Factual and unemotional about problems

6. Non-blaming, non-critical, non-judgmental and non-threatening

c. Ask the **Key Questions** using the following script:

1. What happened in the situation?

2. What do you think went wrong?

3. What did you <u>want</u> to happen?

4. What could <u>you</u> have done differently?

5. Would you be willing to try different choices?

6. *May I help you with those choices?*

d. Proceed to Step 5 **only** if the person answered "Yes" to #5 and #6 above. In the unlikely event of a negative response, see the appropriate section in Chapter 7 for handling the situation.

## Step 5: Traveling from Point A to Point B

A. Obtain the person's commitment to attempt and practice the new choices of behavior in the problem situation.

B. he behavior trials are to be made in the same order as written in the blank staircase spaces leading from Point A to Point B on the map. In the example shown in Figure 6-2, above, for the person needing to replace Parts # 4, 5, and 6, the behavior trials are conducted in that order, including previous acceptable parts, i.e.

1st Trials - Parts #1, 2, 3 + **Part #4**

2nd Trials - Parts #1, 2, 3, 4 + **Part #5**

3rd Trials - Parts #1, 2, 3, 4, 5 **+ Part #6**

C. After each trial, give the proper feedback using the following guidelines:

1. As soon as practical after each behavior trial

2. Use the same setting guidelines as for Step 4

D. Important coaching behaviors during meeting:

1. Warm, caring, etc. and *positive. No negatives, or criticisms*

2. Informal, relaxed and prepared

3. Reflect positive feelings

E. Follow the script in the exact order given below:

**1A, B, C** (Person's name), you did well. I'm proud of you and the (result and/or skill and/or effort) of your new choice.

**2** (Person's name), your new choice really made a difference in how things turned out.

**3A** (Person's name), you should really feel good about yourself for the way that worked out.

(or use the alternative)

**3B** (Person's name), I bet you feel good about yourself for the way that worked out.

F. Using the following codes for feedback and trial results, enter the information for each  behavior trial in the data block for each step on the enlarged map shown as Figure 6-3  on the next page.

**+ means there was a positive trial**

**- means there was a negative trial**

**IA means feedback statement #1A was used**

**IB means feedback statement #1 B was used**

**2 means feedback statement #2 was used**

**3A means feedback statement #3A was used**

**3B means feedback statement #3B was used**

G. Five (5) successful trials using each part are necessary to reinforce new skills, improve competency and self-confidence using the new behaviors.

When the new behaviors are being used successfully, *celebrate the person's arrival at Point B!*

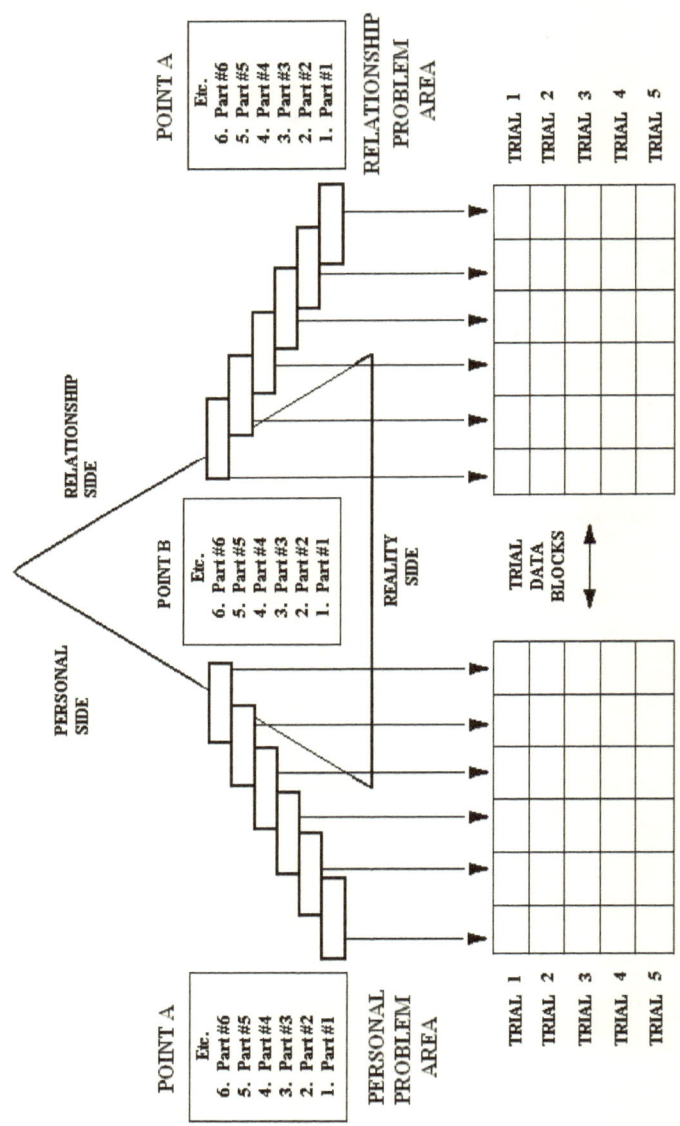

**Figure 6-3 General Behavior Map.**

# Chapter 7

## *Variations with the Method*

### There are always Exceptions

The steps given in this method are general, but will work with most persons having problem behaviors. Since there often will be special conditions, the method has sufficient flexibility to allow for variations. From my experience, the special conditions and variations are in the areas discussed in the following sections.

### Not Yet Ready to Change

Conducting Step 4 using the recommended script order and behaviors usually results in the person answering with a positive response to questions #5 and #6. However, if their answers are negative, they simply may not be ready to change their behaviors. There are three basic causes for this condition:

1. Maintaining the situational problem behaviors is need-fulfilling in other areas of their lives, i.e. more attention from others for the problem behaviors

2. They are in denial of reality, or

3. Others also may need to change

For the first case, if working with children, their need for attention from parents and other adults may be the most important priority. If they can continue to get that attention by acting out, they may not want to give up the problem behaviors until they see that it is no longer **working**. In this situation, the parson giving that attention must reduce/extinguish their response, so that the child's behaviors no longer work successfully to meet that need.

In the second case, the person may not see the need to try different choices because they have an unrealistic attitude about their condition. From their view of reality, they don't perceive that they have a problem that needs changing, and would tend to blame others for the way things turn out. Along with this attitude, there also may be present, albeit on an unconscious level, a belief that things will probably turn out better the next time. Therapists, and other professionals often use this delusion as a "street" definition of insanity:

> *Insanity is repeating the same choices over*
> *and over, and expecting different results.*

While people with this problem are not really insane, they must be helped to see and understand that using the same choices in a situation will always give the same result. When they begin to see their problem in the same way as everyone else in their world, they are on their way to accepting the need for change.

There is a suggested script for this general area of not being ready to change. Starting with **Question #5** in Step 4, the conversation would be as follows for a negative response:

**Coach:** Would you be willing to try different choices?
**Person:** No.
**Coach:** (Person 's name,) don't you think there is a problem?
**Person:** No.
**Coach:** Well, let's say you keep making the same choices. What do you think will happen?
**Person:** I don't know.
**Coach:** From my experience, I think you'll probably get the same results. What do you think?
**Person:** Yeah, maybe.

If they still disagree at this point, then the script continues in a more confrontational way that can break through their resistance to accepting *shared reality.*

**Coach:** (Person 's name,) you may not agree with my opinion about needing different choices, but would you agree if I told you that your teachers, friend's parents, friends, etc. all say the same things? (Use names.)

**Person:** I don't know. I guess so. What did they say?

**Coach:** (Repeat the information as factually as possible.)

If the person still does not agree at this point, then they may need some time to process all that has been said. Allow them that time, but leave them with a final thought about their *unrealistic* attitude.

**Coach:** You know, (Person 's name,) there is a saying that you might think about in trying to decide about working on new choices. It goes something like this,

> *"If one person says you have a tail, you can ignore it, but if many say you have a tail, then maybe you should turn around and look."*

Why don't you think about what we've talked about, and let me know when you want to try something different. If you decide to try some other choices, will you let me help?

**Child:** Yeah, I guess.

## Others Also May Need to Change

Although this subject was introduced in the above section as another possible cause for when someone is not ready for change, it is discussed here as a separate section. When working with children with problem behaviors, it is often the discovered that they are only reacting to the behaviors of others, including parents, other adults, siblings, or peers. When this is the case, changing the child's behaviors may not be possible until the stressors caused by the other person(s) can be changed.

If it is suspected that others could be a factor, learning the conditions and their importance to the child may be accomplished by using the following questions as additions to the Step 4 script:

The original Step 4 Script:

1. What happened in the situation?

2. What do you think went wrong?

3. What did you <u>want</u> to happen?

4. What could <u>you</u> have done differently?

5. Would you be willing to try different choices?

6. May I help you with those choices?

## Additions to the Step 4 Script:

*7. Are there some changes that others in your life could make that would help you be successful with your different choices?*

*8. What are the changes and who would have to make them?*

The credibility of the child's answers to these questions must be carefully weighed. If a parent, or other adult is named and the information is credible, then they would have to be assessed for participation in developing a plan to change. Obviously, if there are conditions caused by others that inhibit the child, they would have to be removed in order for the child to be successful.

The situation with Janine is a good example. During her conversation with the coach in Chapter 4, she said,

**"Everyone always tells me what to do at home and everywhere!"**

Discussions with her parents revealed that Janine was right. She was not given choices at home -- not even in her own bedroom while playing alone! After a conversation with her parents about the importance of allowing her to be *in control in some parts of her world*, there was a general improvement in both her attitude and behaviors in the home. Only when they changed their behaviors by letting her be the "boss" in her own room and other appropriate areas of her world, was Janine willing to let go of trying to be the boss in other places and situations where it was inappropriate.

## What can be Tolerated

As a family therapist, some of my most successful cases were resolved during parent-child meetings based on a simple **key question**:

*If you can't have exactly what you want in the situation, what would you be willing to settle for, or accept?*

Generally, both parents and children were willing to relax their demands of each other enough to agree to negotiate and compromise. This practical approach to problem-solving plays an important role in Steps 4 and 5 of this method.

The above key question about what can be tolerated by the child may be significant in Step # 4 if the child's answer to question #8 involved changes that would be unacceptable without mediation.

For example, if, asking a child question #8:

**What are the changes and who would have to make them?**

the child's response was,

**Mom and dad, can never come into my room, etc,**

then the logical follow-up question using this approach, would be:

**If you can't have that, would you be willing to settle for their knocking on your door first for permission to enter your room?**

For Step #5, the above key question is useful to negotiate the new choices if the child is unwilling to accept the exact behavior parts listed at Point B. With this flexibility in the methodology, coaches are able to suggest new, *negotiable* choices that would gradually lead to the required parts of the behavior in the situation.

Again, it should be mentioned that, although much of this discussion has centered around children as the person needing the changes, the flexibility, approach and additional questions are not limited to that population. It was often very effective when working with couples having relationship issues.

## The 3rd Party Helper

When working with children and others with special needs, it commonly occurs that the parents are unable to detach from strong negative feelings about their child's history with problem behaviors. If those feelings can't be overcome, they will not be successful using this method. Fortunately, parents are not the only persons who can effectively coach their children using the method. Another adult with a personal interest in the child's welfare can act in that role as long as the parents are supportive of the needs of the program. For a third party to help by acting as the coach, the requirements are the same as for parents:

1.  The relationship between the adult and child must be based on **trust**, **caring**, and include a minimum level of **respect**.
2.  The adult must be seen by the child as **competent/credible** to help.
3.  The adult must be seen as **trustworthy**, i.e. will not reveal information shared by the child in confidence without their permission and knowledge.

When children begin to change while working with a third party helper, parents are usually able to reconcile their feelings and attitudes about the past to be included at some level of participation.

## Other Professionals as Helpers

In many children's lives, there are professionals viewed as strong authority figures, such as teachers, doctors, etc. who also may be successful in the role of third party helpers, if they can be enlisted for this activity. Since they may be unfamiliar with this 5-STEP method for coaching to change behaviors, the following procedure is recommended for the first contact with such a person.

I.   Ask for their confidentiality about anything you may tell them about the child.

II.  Tell them of your concern about the child's direction and development due to their problem behaviors.

III. Ask if they have suggestions for helping the child make changes.

IV.  If they do not, ask if they would be willing to participate by using the 5-STEP method while working in their specific area of interaction with the child.

V.   If they support the idea, provide them with the information necessary to use the method.

VI.  As a team effort, communicate frequently to understand what the child is doing in all areas.

## The Very Young

Using the method described in this book with very young children requires several variations. Their capabilities to make sense of the world and to communicate may not be adequately developed for normal interactions based on the required dialogue. The changes needed are in the area of parental participation as *models* in their role as the coach.

The situation for 18-month-old Jason that was given in the beginning of the book is a good example. For his age group, he was expected to safely explore a range of feelings, including such common negative ones as anger and aggression. Typically, those ways of exploration are through fantasy play with appropriate toys and scenarios. Total avoidance and fear of these kinds of feelings would have affected his development.

For helping Jason, his parents followed Steps 1, 2 and 3 in a normal way. Since Jason did not have the ability to participate in Step 4 and parts of Step 5, they had to find ways of introducing the new behavior parts for him to use. By ***modeling*** the new behaviors while coaching during his play, they were able to stimulate Jason to begin responding in expected ways. Those responses were then tracked on his Step 5 behavior map in the same way that feedback and behavior progress is tracked for older children. The feedback scripts used with older children may not work, however, even with this age group, it is very important that they perceive the results, and the attitude of others to be positive in order to reinforce their behaviors during these trials. To properly convey this, the parents/coaches may have to be very creative with their own behaviors!

**Chapter 7 Checklist: Things to remember**

- There will be exceptions to the general types of situations and personalities used here as examples. However, the method is flexible to be adaptable to these challenges

- In some cases, the person may simply not be ready to make the behavior changes that are obvious to everyone around them. This special condition may exist due to one of the reasons listed below

  1. Maintaining the situational problem behaviors is need-fulfilling in other areas      of their lives, i.e. more attention from others for the problem behaviors

  2. They are in denial of reality, or

  3. Others also may need to change

- When others in the person's life must also change, it will complicate the whole process. However, these stressors must be removed before effective change/correction can be achieved. The first step in working within this scenario is to understand who and what is involved.

- Additions to the Step 4 script, as repeated below, will be useful for determining these issues:

  *Are there some changes that others in your life could make that would help you be successful with your different choices?*

  *What are the changes and who would have to make them?*

- Regardless of the wants and needs of everyone involved with the process of changing behaviors, it may often come down to a negotiable situation about what can be "tolerated." When that is the case, then the *realistic* question that must be asked is:

***If you can't have exactly what you want in the situation, what would you be willing to settle for, or accept?***

- Working with very young children will often require the parent/ coach to "model" the behavior desired, rather than use the complete text of the scripts that are so important to those old enough for those kinds of communications. In any event, the feedback must still be perceived as positive and reinforcing for the expected behaviors in the situation addressed.

# Chapter 8

## *Helping the person stay at Point B*

*If Point A behaviors were ever successfully used to get needs or wants met, then they will always be available as a <u>choice</u> to use again.*

### <u>Relapse and Prevention</u>

Now that the coached person has arrived at Point B, you want them to stay there and, hopefully, never again resort to using the old problem behaviors. Unfortunately, any behavior used long enough to become the "norm," and <u>work</u> for the person under certain circumstances, can always be chosen for use again. From this perspective, when such a person is choosing new, improved behaviors, they are in a state of *recovery*, similar to someone recovering from an addictive behavior. (See Appendix A for more details concerning this issue)

Choosing to go back to using old behaviors that were previously unacceptable may only be a onetime occurrence, or it could be a sign of resumed use. When it is total resumed use, it is considered to be a *relapse*. A behavior relapse can be due to different reasons, including the following:

- Insufficient support/reinforcement of the new behaviors
- Exposure to high-risk/stressful situations
- Return of stressors/conditions caused by others

The coach and the person making changes has control over some of these causes, but not all. Therefore, the following suggestions are made for relapse prevention.

## Insufficient Support of New Behavior

Once an individual has made behavior changes, the improved communications and feedback skills that the coach, or parents learned to use in this method <u>must</u> be continued. While the quality of the feedback given is a very important aspect of helping anyone, especially children, develop and maintain new behaviors, it must be maintained, even after the person is well on their way to sustaining the changes.

Remember that, in the early stages of using new behaviors, they will still be somewhat *fragile* when it comes to the type of feedback they receive. Blunt, candid feedback, often acceptable between "evolved," mature adults, can cause problems for many ordinary people, but can be absolutely devastating for those trying to maintain newly learned behaviors that they are still unsure over. In particular, negative, or critical ways of interacting with these persons can send the wrong message with the potential for causing a full blown relapse if their faulty appraisal processes still include:

> *"The only time they pay any attention, or act like they <u>care</u> about me is when I behave in ways that cause problems!"*

It doesn't take much imagination to see that this kind of thinking can quickly lead to a relapse!

To avoid this cause for relapse, coaches and other adults in these person's lives need to maintain high levels of support by continuing to use the basic feedback guidelines in Step 5. During this maintenance stage, neither the order nor the wording are critical, as long as it is *never negative, or critical.* The important rule to use is:

> *If no positive features are available for comment about a person's behaviors, then use <u>descriptive feedback</u>.*

For example, if a person's behaviors were negative in the areas of effect, skill and effort, then use a comment that **describes** anything about the behavior, such as in the following:

(Person's name,) that was a very **cheerful** way you went about doing that!

Of course, depending on the person's age, this kind of comment may be very transparent as feedback, and they may challenge it. If they do challenge it as unrealistic, handle it as if it were really meant. In any case, unconsciously they still process it as positive feedback, so the job gets done! Other important ways for supporting behavior changes, especially with children, are to be as physically and emotionally available to them as when they were working on making changes at the program outset.

## High Risk/Stress Situations

High risk situations are conditions where the persons are strongly tempted to return to using the old behaviors rather than continue the new. Often this occurs when there is a return to specific geographical locations, or social situations where the old behaviors were the norm. For example, if a person used the problem behaviors in the presence of peers with similar problems, they would be likely to choose their old behavior if they wanted to be accepted by this group once again. Therefore, *avoiding* destructive peer group influence may be important for maintaining the new behaviors and preventing relapse.

High stress situations are conditions where the persons experience levels of stress they perceive are overwhelming for their ability to cope, i.e. a crisis. For example, if a close friend has been physically injured, the person would be likely to return to using an old, more "comfortable" behavior. At these times, the most that a coach, or parent can do is be available physically and emotionally for support until the crisis passes, then use the proper feedback for getting the person back on track for functioning at Point B.

## Return of Conditions Caused by others

Unfortunately, some conditions can be due to someone else's behaviors, i.e. over-critical feedback, failure to take an interest in the person's life, relationship strife, etc. While coaches may not always have control over this cause for relapse, increased vigilance in this area could prevent problems. By warning the person that the possibility exists for this situation to occur and suitably processing it, may be sufficient for prevention.

From my experience with children, various stressful conditions are caused by the behaviors of other adults, siblings, or peers in the child's life. The first understanding of the importance of any these problem areas may come during Step 4 when additional questions #7 and #8 are used. From that knowledge, parents/coaches can plan what to do if they recur and threaten the child's ability to maintain their changed behaviors.

## Chapter 8 Checklist: Things to remember

- Relapse occurs if the person **chooses** to resume using a problem behavior pattern – regardless of the cause!

- Relapse can be due to insufficient support of new behaviors, return of the conditions caused by others, or high-risk/stressful situations
- Relapse prevention is an important part of staying at Point B
- During the early stages of maintaining the behavior changes, feedback doesn't have to follow a scripted dialogue, as long as it is *never negative, or critical.* The following rule applies in all cases:

> ***If no positive features are available for comment about the person's behaviors, then use <u>descriptive feedback</u>.***

- An example of simple descriptive feedback is,

(Person's name,) that was a very **cheerful** way you went about doing that!

# Chapter 9

## *A Complete Example*

### Tiffany's Tantrums

Tiffany was the 4-year-old of a single, working mother forced to leave her at a nursery every weekday. She frequently threw tantrums, leaving everyone drained for the remainder of the day. Tiffany's difficulties with the daily separation were understandable, however, at her age, she was **expected to have some capacity to cope** with this type of frustration. Tiffany's mother basically knew that her daughter should have been coping differently, but did not have the information, nor support for helping her change her behaviors.

### Step 1: What is Tiffany Actually Doing?

The problem behaviors selected by her mother primarily occurred at the nursery. However, when asked to describe Tiffany's actual behaviors so that **LIST A** could be made, it was determined that Tiffany's problematic behaviors first began in the mornings at home.

Her mother first described on paper the following sequence of events:

> Tiffany sits quietly and watches cartoons. After several prompts, she does gather her stuff to take to school. Once in the car, she fusses all the way about having to go. When they arrive, she is rude and unpleasant to everyone. When I have to leave for work, she usually throws a major tantrum. Finally, her teacher reports that her behaviors were uncooperative for doing most of their activities during the day.

This information from Tiffany's mother converts to the following LIST A of Tiffany's actual behavior parts:

## LIST A – TIFFANY'S ACTUAL BEHAVIORS

Behavior Part #1 - Sits quietly and watches cartoons until Mom's ready
Behavior Part #2 - Gets stuff together for the day
Behavior Part #3 - Gets in car and fusses on the way
Behavior Part #4 - Doesn't greet nicely
Behavior Part #5 - Has tantrum
Behavior Part #6 - Won't cooperate

This simple list is now ready to be added to Tiffany's map as **Point A**, but her mother needed to know on what side of the triangle it was located. The side of the behavior map where the problem behaviors would be located was identified by the answer to the question:

> *Is the effect of Tiffany's behavior mainly in the area of her relationships with others, in the area of her personal functioning, or in her view of reality?*

Her mother's answer to this question was, "mainly in the area of her relationships with others," so Tiffany's actual behaviors, LIST A, could now be placed on the **relationship side** of the Behavior Map. Next, her mother was asked if Tiffany's behaviors were closer to the "Isolation" or the "Engulfed" endpoint on the Relationship side. Like Janine, her behaviors were determined to be in the direction of the **Isolated** endpoint, but not quite so close to the endpoint. While her behaviors did have the effect of causing others to distance themselves from her when she was acting out, it did not have the same effect with her ability to make friends and play with others, i.e. her behaviors were not the same as Janine's that prevented her from playing with anyone.

Following the correct procedure for this step, when written on the **Point A** data block, the LIST A parts are written in an inverted order, with Part 1 at the bottom of the block and Part 6 at the top of the block. The Point A List entry is given on the partial map shown in Figure 9-1.

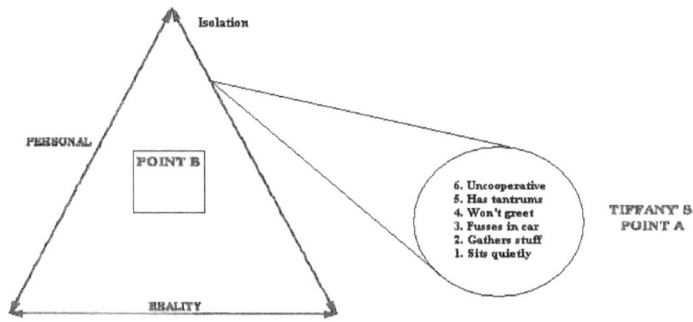

**Figure 9-1 Tiffany's partial behavior map showing her Point A location and list.**

## Step 2: What should Tiffany be doing?

Next, on paper, her mother wrote how Tiffany's behaviors and their mornings should be like.

> Tiffany would sit quietly after breakfast and watch cartoons on the T.V. until Mom is about ready to leave. Next, she would gather the things she needs for her day at the nursery, such as her coat, doll and favorite blanket, and they would get in the car. Tiffany would behave in the car on the way to school, and greet everyone nicely once they arrive. When Mom is ready to leave, Tiffany would be nice about it. Further, she would stay nice and cooperate with her teacher until picked up by her mother at the end of the day.

When her mother's ideas of what Tiffany <u>should</u> be doing were converted to form LIST B of Tiffany's expected behavior parts, it appears as the following:

### LIST B – TIFFANY'S EXPECTED BEHAVIORS

Part #1 - Sit quietly and watch cartoons until Mom's ready
Part #2 - Get stuff together for the day, i.e. toys, blanket, etc
Part #3 - Get in car and behave o.k. on the way
Part #4 - Greet others nicely
Part #5 - Stay calm when Mom has to leave for work
Part # 6 - Cooperate with teachers until Mom returns

This list was then written in inverted order in the data block at **Point B** on the partial map shown in Figure 9-2

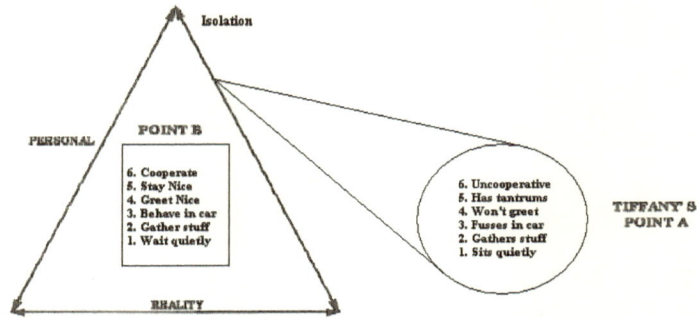

**Figure 9-2 Tiffany's Point A Behaviors and the Point B list of behaviors.**

### Step 3: Comparing Behavior Lists and Choices

Next, it was time for Tiffany's mother to <u>compare</u> the List A of actual behaviors at Point A with the List B of expected behaviors at Point B for the situation. In this Step, it was necessary to identify any behavior parts at Point A not closely matched to the same parts listed at Point B. Tiffany's Step 3 Behavior map, shown in Figure 9-3, is a larger format provided for easier data entry.

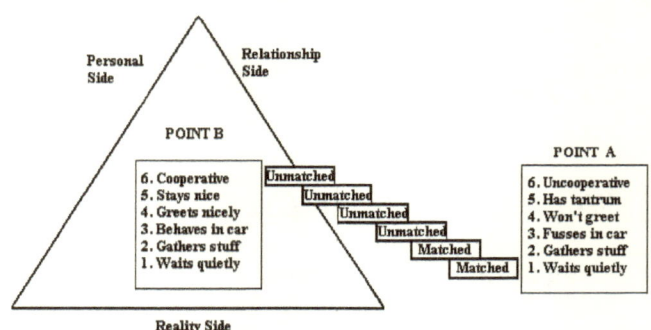

**Figure 9-3 Tiffany's Behavior Map at Step 3.**

For the parts identified as "unmatched," her mother selected new choices for Tiffany and wrote them in the spaces leading towards Point B. Her selections took into consideration the following:

> **a. *Tiffany's wants and needs in the situation***
> **b. *Point B behavior,* and**
> **c. *Information from other sources,* i.e. teachers, etc.**

To understand Tiffany's **wants and needs** in the situation, her mother thought about their hectic and, often, impersonal life style. As a working, single parent there was no personal time available for Tiffany during the day, and very little in the evenings because of routine household tasks and low energy. As a result, Tiffany seemed to do everything she could to stay close to her mother when they were together, including throwing tantrums. With some insight from me on this issue, it became obvious to her mother that what Tiffany really wanted <u>and</u> needed was quality time, rather than only the time spent together on task-related activities.

The parts listed previously for Point B behaviors were retained as target selections by her mother in this part of the method because they were appropriate choices for the nursery school situation at Tiffany's age. However, variations on these choices were acceptable as options, as long as they were effective and remained appropriate.

Because Tiffany's mother did not have enough time with her daughter to really know everything about her daily activities and valued interests, she spoke with the teacher at school. She learned that Tiffany's behavior always temporarily improved during story time, or when singing songs.

All of this information, i.e. Tiffany's **wants and needs**, **Point B behavior** and **information from others** helped her mother arrive at a plan for proceeding. This plan included the idea of linking the Point B target choices with Tiffany's wants/needs and favorite interests (those she valued the most.) As planned, it would work in the following way:

- Offer Tiffany the choice of telling stories or singing songs while riding in the car on the way to school, **only if** she was willing to make the different behavior choices at Point B, i.e.:
  - No fussing in the car
  - Greeting everyone nicely, and
  - Staying calm/nice when Mom has to leave, i.e. no tantrums

- Failure to make the new behavior choices would stop the activities until Tiffany was ready to begin again.

If Tiffany goes along with this plan, the 1st unmatched part, **fussing in the car**, would be directly corrected. Furthermore, the 2nd and 3rd parts would be corrected indirectly if Tiffany placed enough value on the new quality time activity with her mother to repeat the new choices again each day.

Notice that the new choices did not include the last part of Point B, being **cooperative**. That part will naturally be corrected as a result of Tiffany's other changes. If class cooperation remains the only unmatched part, it could be addressed separately after progress is made in the area of her school arrival behaviors. It is important that children do not feel overwhelmed by suggesting too many changes at one time.

This plan was formally completed when Tiffany's mother wrote the new choices in the blank spaces on the map shown as Figure 9-4 on the next page.

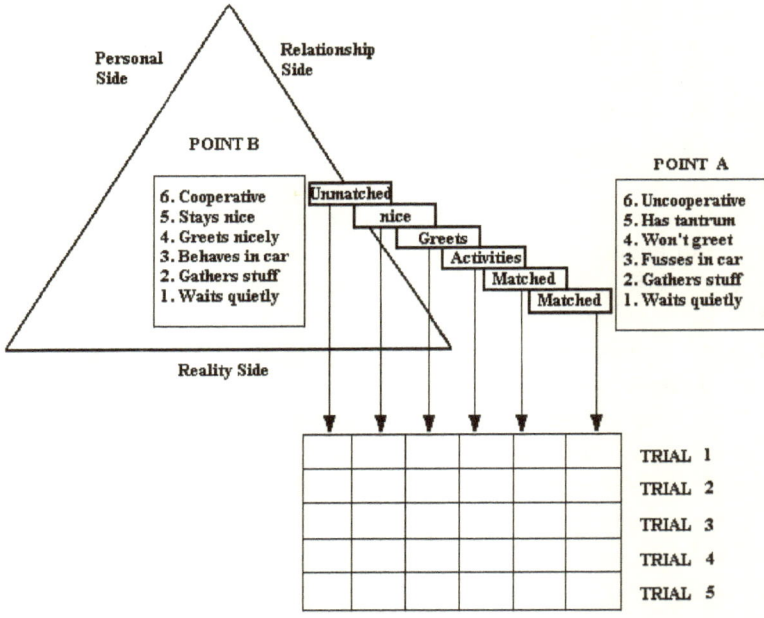

**Figure 9-4 Tiffany's Behavior Map at Step 3 showing the new choices.**

Once **Step 3** was completed, it was time to involve Tiffany in the process.

### Step 4: The beginning of Change

Her mother, acting in the role of the <u>coach</u>, understood that she needed to meet with Tiffany in the proper setting and use the proper behavior towards her. (Refer to Chapter 4 for the guidelines.) They sat down in her bedroom after dinner one evening, told others not to interrupt and closed the door for privacy. Following the *script*, her mother asked the **key questions** (shown below in bold print) to get Tiffany's commitment to change. Since her mother was now fully trained to be the coach during this time, she will only be referred to as "**Coach**" in all of the following dialog..

**Coach:** What happened when we got to your school today, do you remember?

**Tiffany:** Yes.

**Coach:** What? What did you do?

**Tiffany:** I made you upset.

**Coach:** What do you think went wrong to cause that?

**Tiffany:** I fussed.

**Coach:** What did you want to happen?

**Tiffany:** I didn't want you to go.

**Coach:** But, Tiffany, you know Mommy has to go to work. That's my job. Your job is to be there, cooperate with the teachers to learn what they have to teach you, and behave yourself until I come back to pick you up, right?

**Tiffany:** Yeah.

**Coach:** What could you have done differently?

**Tiffany:** I don't know.

**Coach:** Well, tell you what, when I take you tomorrow, how about we try something new, so we don't have that same problem? Are you willing to try something different?

**Tiffany:** I guess so. What?

**Coach:** Well, you like stories and singing songs when we're riding in the car, don't you?

**Tiffany:** Yeah!

**Coach:** Well, then let's make a deal. We can either tell stories, or sing in the car on the way. It'll be your choice. All you have to do is make some different choices about your behavior, starting with not fussing in the car along the way, being nice when you get to school and, especially, when I leave. Okay? Would you be willing to try those new choices?

**Tiffany:** Okay, I'll try. But I don't like doing their dumb stuff at school. They make us clean up the whole place and everything after we play! It's too hard. Will you tell me a story now?

**Coach:** Okay, but just a short one 'cause it's your bedtime.

Notice that in this situation, Tiffany's mother <u>did not use</u> the following script options:

* **Key Question #6** about helping Tiffany with her different choices, because at this stage, it was unnecessary.

* **Optional Key Questions #7 & #8**, about changes others could make, because at Tiffany's age, she may not have been able to identify the problem.

## Step 5: Traveling from Point A to Point B.

Following the guidelines given for Step 5, her mother knew that she had to *confirm* Tiffany's commitment to try the new choices. Then they could actually have the first behavior trial. The next morning, as they got into the car, her mother asked her if she remembered their conversation the night before. Tiffany said that she did and had already decided she wanted to hear the story about Cinderella. Her mother reminded her of the "deal" she agreed to during their talk. She said she did, and the story was told.

By the time they arrived at school, both were in a much better mood than usual. To everyone's surprise, Tiffany was pleasant and greeted her teacher and peers very nicely when they went inside.

Although Tiffany did pout when it was time for her mother to leave, there was not the normal tantrum, or other upsetting incident for the first time since she started attending this school.

At the end of the day, her Mother spoke to the teacher and learned Tiffany had had a much better day than usual. Although she could still improve in the area of doing what she was told, this was a good start. While riding in the car on the way home, Tiffany's mother used the Step 5 *script to give important feedback*. At the end of each scripted feedback statement, the Feedback Code is given in parenthesis to assist the reader with this identification.

Coach:  **Tiffany, you did very well** this morning in the car and when we got to school.
**I'm proud of you and the result of your new choice.** (This was Feedback Code lA.)

Tiffany:  Uh huh.

Coach:  **Your new choice really made a difference in how things turned out,** don't you think? (This was Feedback Code 2.)

Tiffany:  Yeah, even Stephanie was nice to me after you left!

Coach:  Wow, that's great, **Tiffany. You should really feel good about yourself for the way everything worked out this morning**. (This was Feedback Code 3A.)

**Tiffany:**   Uh huh. Tomorrow morning can you tell me the story about Jack in the Beanstock?

**Coach:**   Sure, if that's what you choose.

Later that night, she updated Tiffany's behavior map with the data for the 1st trial. This was done by entering the results of the trial and the feedback codes used. The codes used were as stated in Step 5, i.e.

> \+ means there was a positive trial
> \- means there was a negative trial
> 1A means feedback statement #1 A was used
> 1B means feedback statement #1 B was used
> 2 means feedback statement #2 was used
> 3A means feedback statement #3A was used
> 3B means feedback statement #3 B was used

At the end of each trial, these codes were written in the spaces directly under the new behavior choices that were tried. When more than one choice was involved, the space for the last one was the one used for that data, as used on Tiffany's map shown in Figure 9-5.

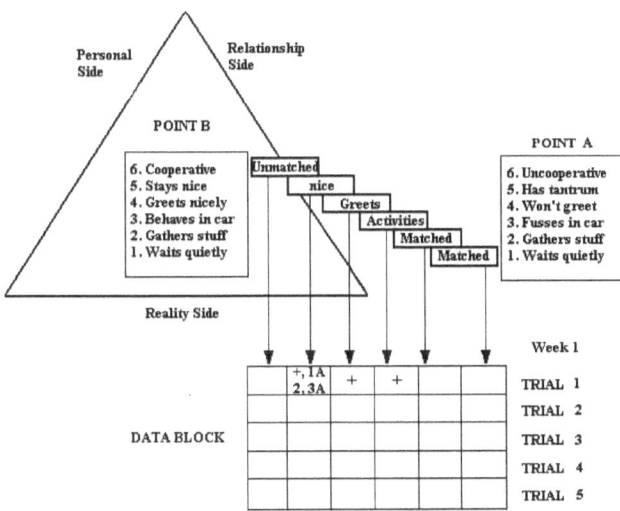

**Figure 9-5 Tiffany's Behavior Map for Step 5 showing data points for Trial 1.**

The car activity for behavior Part #3 was repeated for the week, with the same positive results for the 2nd, 4th and 5th trials. For the 3rd trial, Tiffany had a very bad day from the start. She fussed in the car and was horrid when she got to school. In other words, she was experiencing a partial **relapse** because she had reverted back to using her old habitual behavior pattern. Since the trial was negative, *no feedback* statements were used.

When Tiffany did not get her special activity on the way to school the following day, she complained, but was reminded of her choices the day before. After thinking about it for awhile, she asked if she could start again for the next day. Her mother agreed and Tiffany remained quiet on the way to school.

The behavior map at Step 5 with all data for the first week is shown as Figure 9-6. Notice that the feedback statements used were varied from day-to-day. This kept the scripted messages from sounding too "canned" and obvious to the person involved in changing behaviors.

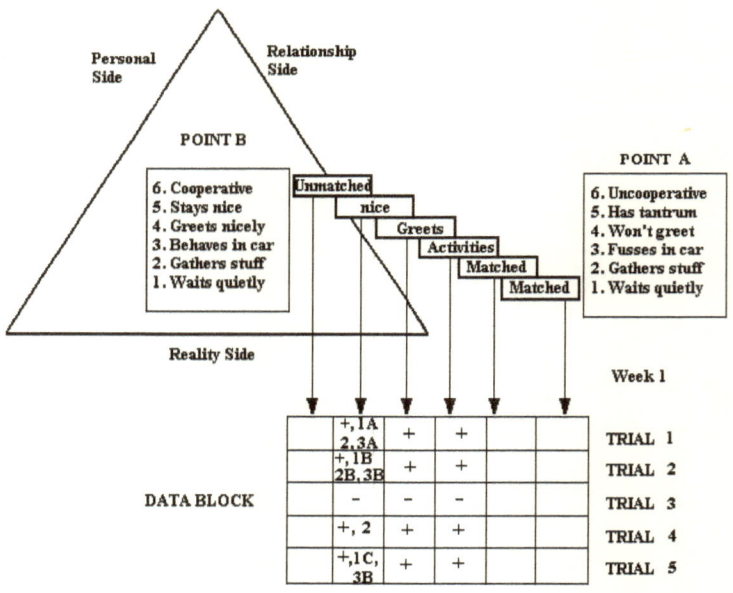

**Figure 9-6 Tiffany's Behavior Map at Step 5 showing the trial data for Week 1.**

Tiffany did so well that by the end of the first week, her behaviors at school were acceptable to everyone. However, she continued to be unco-operative about some of the tasks, such as putting things away, cleaning up, etc. Since Tiffany had had such a successful week, her mother thought the time was right to begin the next correction.

Using the same basic idea of offering Tiffany quality time as an incentive for change, her mother decided to give her 20 minutes every night for reading books, etc. when she had good reports from the teacher about being cooperative during the day. It would be up to Tiffany to get this additional time with her mother by **choosing** to be cooperative. When this idea was presented by the script of Step 5, Tiffany enthusiastically agreed and said she would try to be cooperative.

The second week went well with positive trials for all areas. The data for Tiffany's final Step 5 behavior map is shown as Figure 9-7.

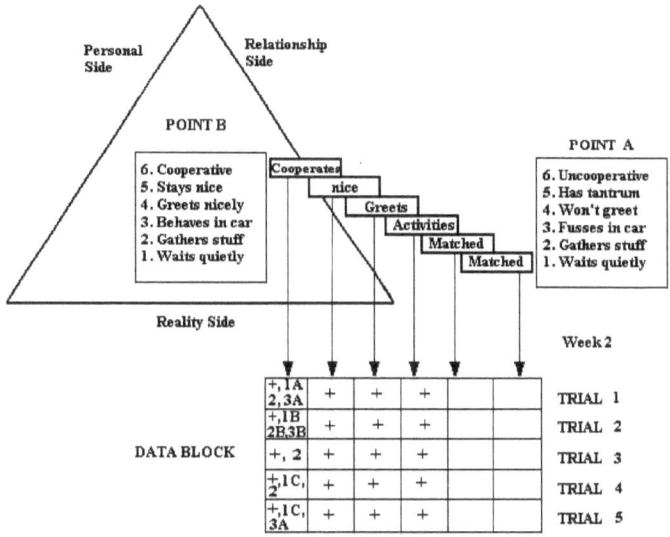

**Figure 9-7 Tiffany's Behavior Map at Step 5 showing the trial data for Week 2.**

### After the Correction

Since Tiffany had achieved at least five positive behavior trials with the different choices, she had successfully completed the correction that her mother and others had wanted for her in the nursery school situation. After only two weeks, she was using the expected behaviors of Point B as well as any of the other children.

To help Tiffany maintain her changes, and prevent a behavior relapse, her mother kept the incentives in place, while continuing the same level of communications and feedback techniques used in the 5-STEP method for all of her behaviors. Eventually, Tiffany lost interest in the story-telling car activity and was content to simply talk about different things on the way to school. At that point, her mother began to link her nursery school behaviors to the highly-valued quality time that came at the end of each day.

Tiffany was able to maintain the expected nursery school behaviors without further serious problems. However, as with any child of that age, she had her good days and bad days. On the bad days, loss of the special time with her mother was always enough of a consequence to motivate her for making better choices the following day.

An enlarged version of the complete general map shown earlier, is now provided to the reader/coach as Figure 9-8 for general use on the next page.

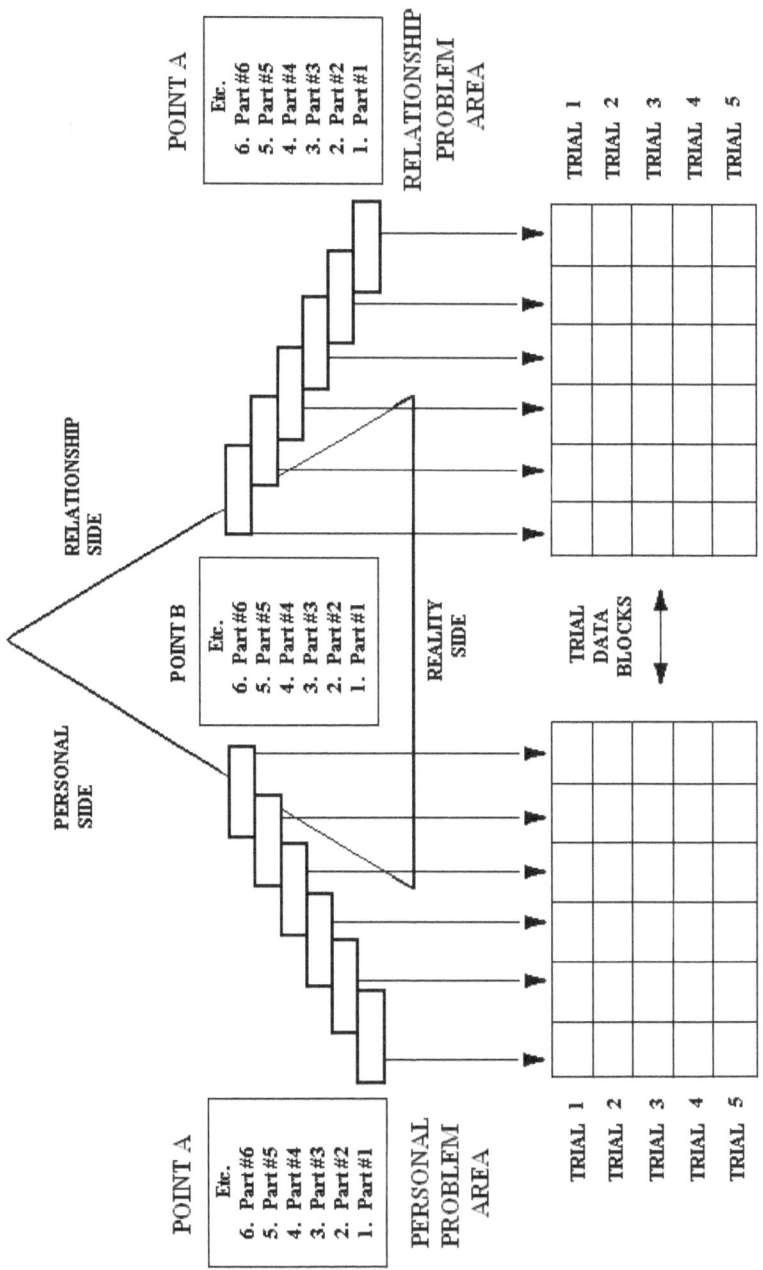

**Figure 9-8 General Behavior Map.**

# Chapter 10

## *Postscript: The Model*

### A Bird's Eye View

So far I have done my best to avoid having this book read like a textbook.

As mentioned earlier in the introduction, I understand that most parents and adults acting as coaches are not interested in how a method works, but only that it <u>does</u> work and how it is actually applied, or practiced to be useful. For those who do have some interest in the theory behind the model, a brief view may be helpful. More information is available in the Appendix, and more may be provided in a future textbook-like publication if there is sufficient interest.

### Design of the Steps

Each of the steps is a practical *activity* that is performed in a particular sequence, similar to the way certain kinds of puzzles have to be put together. In this section, the basis and importance of each step will be described to show how they fit together, and to help interested readers make sense of it all.

### Step 1

The task for identifying the parts of Point A is at the beginning of the method for several reasons. Firstly, it focuses on the problem behaviors in the most realistic and concrete way, i.e. "What is really going on?" Secondly, it introduces the coach to the practice of observation and analysis of the separate, logical parts making up any situational behavior. Just as importantly, by focusing on this analytical way of looking at behaviors, it prepares the coach for detaching from the normal personal feelings and attitudes about the person's actual behaviors. Without this objectivity, some coaches, and most parents, cannot effectively assist another person to make the necessary changes. When completed correctly, Step 1 provides the foundation block around which all others are built.

Because this step questions at the outset precisely what one is actually doing in the particular situation, this step has its basis in the therapeutic modality of Reality Therapy.

### Step 2

Step 2 is the activity for identifying the behaviors expected in any similar social situation within the culture. By the time that coaches perform this step, they have had some understanding and practice of breaking down behaviors into their small, separate parts. Listing different parts of the expected behaviors at Point B is made easier because they have already made the Point A list and anticipate that a parts comparison will be made in a future step. Because the Point B information should include the needs and wants of the person in the particular situation, the basis for this step is also in the therapeutic modalities of **Reality Therapy** and **Esteem Therapy**.

Information concerning the Esteem Therapy model is located in Appendix A of this text.

### Step 3

The final activity that coaches must complete before working directly with the person needing behavior change is Step 3, where each of the parts of the Point A list are compared, on a one-to-one basis, with each of the corresponding parts of the Point B list. In this step, coaches are specifically looking for all *deviations between the actual behavior parts and the expected, or standard behavior parts* for this type of social situation in the culture. Actual parts that deviate enough to cause problems for the person, or others, are the parts that must be addressed and replaced. Obviously, the replacements, that will be used to create a new list, should resemble, as closely as possible, the parts listed at Point B for that specific action. However, until the person actually participates in the process, the coach should only "pencil-in" the new choices. Step 3, identifying the parts needing to be replaced, in fact becomes the "action plan" for proceeding towards change.

### Step 4

In Step 4, the person with the problem behaviors is finally involved in the process. From the activity at Step 3, coaches now *know* the behavior parts needing replacement. By following the scripted key questions, the person is guided/cued to choose the new parts that most closely match those at Point B. Step 4 is complete when they commit to actually trying the parts shown on the staircase leading from Point A to Point B. Thus, the separate parts involved in Step 4 *reflect* the person's commitment to try the parts previously selected on a tentative basis by the coach at Step 3. Making this important commitment, to try new choices of behavior to replace those not working well, also has its basis in Reality Therapy, as well as other modalities.

## Step 5

Step 5 is the last building block necessary to complete the activity we have been developing, or assembling. At this final step, the person should be performing a series of behavior trials that begin with the first part to be changed, i.e. the lowest step on the staircase, and progress towards the highest step. As success is experienced, competence and confidence grows, and the remaining replacement parts are added as new trials. Step 5 is accomplished through the coach's important use of *feedback scripts* to guide and/or reinforce the person's new behavior choices during and after each of the different behavior trials.

The basis for this step is in the therapeutic modality, **Esteem Therapy**, founded by this author and applied extensively with many populations. Information concerning the Esteem Therapy model and its applications with adolescents is located in Appendix A of this text.

### Source Materials and References

The preparation of this book was the result of many years of formal education and training, personal studies, and ultimate applications as a private practitioner and contract therapist/counselor for the State of Arizona (Department of Juvenile Corrections and Department of Economic Security). Consequently, the references and source material used to develop the methods disclosed in this document are too numerous to list in the fields of counseling, psychology and sociology. However, two texts of significance to this work were the following:

1. Glasser, William, MD., *Reality Therapy: A New Approach to Psychiatry*, foreword by O.H. Mowrer, Ph.D., Harper and Row, NY, 1965.

2. Glasser, William, MD., *Mental Health or Mental Illness*, Harper and Row, 1960.

3. Marlatt, G. A., & Gordon, J. R. (Eds.), *Relapse prevention*, New York: Guilford Press, 1985.

# APPENDIX A

## *Results of the Esteem Therapy Substance Abuse Treatment Model for Juvenile Offenders*

**A SPECIAL REPORT**

**for the**

**STATE OF ARIZONA**

July 1990

Prepared in support of
Arizona Department of Corrections
Professional Services Contract
# DC-J/CS-SUBAB-88/91-4146
by

**Jack W. Scannell, M.A.**

Founder of Esteem Therapy,
Certified Reality Therapist,
Chemical Dependency Counselor

# Contents

# Section A-I

## *Introduction And Purpose*

The Esteem Therapy (ET) substance abuse treatment program was selected in 1988 by the State of Arizona as a new model to be implemented and evaluated for juveniles committed to the Department of Corrections. To accomplish that goal, Jack Scannell, the proposer and developer of this model, was awarded fixed price Professional Services Contract #DC-J/CS-SUBAB-88/9l-4l46 **to provide institutional intervention services and community-based support services to both male and female juvenile offenders at various locations in the State of Arizona.**

The purpose of this special document is to report some of the results of the use of the Esteem Therapy substance abuse treatment model as it was successfully applied to 108 cases from November 1, 1988 to June 30, 1990. Some of the most important results from the analysis of the cases treated in this program are as follows:

1. Of the 98 cases eligible for substance abuse recovery measurement/ observation following the institution intervention treatment phase of the program, approximately 85 percent successfully maintained some form of recovery. Approximately 15 percent experienced a full relapse.

2.  Approximately 90 percent of the females treated for substance abuse in this program were also treated for sexual abuse issues using the Esteem Therapy victim abuse model.

3.  Approximately 87 percent of the total population treated in this program experienced significant self-esteem improvements.

4.  High intensity therapeutic institution intervention services may preclude the need for regular professional community support services, based on the comparable recovery results for a segment of the population that experienced that variation.

5.  Of the 98 cases eligible for institutional recidivism measurement/ observation following completion of the institution intervention treatment phase of the program, approximately 26 percent were observed to return to the institution prior to turning 18.

6.  The predicted national and State of Arizona juvenile institution recidivism rate in 1988 was about 65 percent. The lower recidivism rate observed for the population treated in this program conceivably translates into an estimated minimum cost savings for the State of Arizona that amounts to over $433,000 during the 21 months this program was conducted.

Details of these and other findings are included in this report.

# Section A-II

## *The Esteem Therapy Substance Abuse Treatment Model*

The model implemented for this program was based on the principles of Esteem Therapy (ET), a psychological treatment approach founded by the provider, Jack Scannell, in 1987. The specific application of those principles to the general substance abuse problem area for various recovering populations provided the following premises for this model:

A. Many of the underlying psychological stressors commonly linked to low self-esteem are also important causative factors in the development and progression of substance-using behaviors.

B. The prolonged effects of substance abuse behavior patterns include serious damage to the self-esteem.

C. Successful recovery from substance abuse behaviors must be based on a holistic, multi-modal process that includes treating the underlying psychological stressors, the behaviors and the self-esteem.

D. The process of "balanced" substance abuse recovery contains important aspects that are parallel to many of the processes associated with the healthy emotional development of the self.

E. The individual's commitment to the treatment program for recovery requires the existence of a motivational state to change.

F.　Creation of that motivational state to change requires a minimum level of self-esteem in each person.

G.　Development and maintenance of that minimum level of self-esteem must be accomplished during the intervention phase of the treatment program to effectively motivate, engage and empower the person in the process of change.

H.　Development and maintenance of the minimum level of self-esteem is facilitated by the **Esteem Therapist** acting as a **coach** to provide appropriate motivation, empowerment, support, guidance and feedback during all stages of the process.

I.　Correction of structural self-esteem defects related to underlying stressors, new growth of self-esteem from the minimum level and the emotional development of the self must be addressed by the **Esteem Therapist** during all stages of treatment to facilitate successful maintenance of balanced substance abuse recovery, and prevention of relapse.

J.　Successful application of the Esteem Therapy model will facilitate and address the recovery from related issues that often accompany substance abuse, such as codependency, eating disorders, sexual disorders and abusive behaviors towards others.

# Section A-III

## *Program Goals*

### TREATMENT MODEL GOALS

From the principles used in describing the basis for the substance abuse treatment model, the primary therapeutic goals were defined as:

1.  Facilitate the development and maintenance of a minimum level of self-esteem sufficient to motivate, empower and support the individual to commit to entering and engaging in substance abuse treatment for interrupting the substance use/abuse progression and developing a unique sustainable program of recovery. To accomplish this goal, the Esteem Therapist often acts in the role of a "**coach**" to assist the recovering person.

2.  Correct self-esteem structural defects and promote the growth of authentic self-esteem from the minimum level sufficiently to facilitate successful maintenance of a program of recovery that includes decreasing the use of, or maintaining abstinence from drugs/alcohol, and the prevention of relapse. To accomplish this goal the Esteem Therapist acts in the dual roles of both psychological **therapist and coach**.

3.  Treat the total recovery needs of the individual using a holistic and eclectic approach to facilitate successful, long-term balanced functioning in the community.

A secondary treatment model goal considered important by the provider was also included.

4.  Determine the long term effects of the application of the Esteem Therapy (ET) substance abuse treatment model using a population sample size sufficiently large to provide meaningful data evaluation. Compare with trends previously observed.

Although the above model goals are stated with the specific program focus on treatment and recovery from substance abuse for juvenile offenders, the three primary treatment goals and means to accomplish are consistent with the general goals of Esteem Therapy (ET), regardless of the presenting recovery problem, or age of the population. Since the program included institution and community support components, successful goal achievement was expected to depend upon the overall capability to provide a continuum approach to the delivery of child and mental health care services. As this model was based on a comprehensive therapeutic methodology with goals and capabilities that exceeded those related to recovery from a single problem area, the proposed approach was predicted to be successful in providing that continuum.

The purpose of the secondary goal was to increase the level of confidence for using the treatment model based on the Esteem Therapy methodology. Since that required long term applications and observations of large sample sizes, successful achievement of that goal was expected to be the program outcome, provided that the model could be rigorously and consistently applied for a reasonably large population sample size for an extended period of time in various environmental settings. This program provided the first opportunity to accomplish that goal.

## STATE PURCHASING AGENCY GOALS

In addition to the goals defined for the substance abuse treatment model by the provider, various other goals were defined and mandated in contract form by the appropriate State purchasing agency. The agency charged with that responsibility for this program was the Purchase of Care unit of the Arizona Department of Corrections.

Since the goals required by contract were numerous and located in various State reference documents, only a summary of the most important ones, as determined by the provider, are presented here. Copies of the specific guidelines can be obtained from the program scope section of RFP #4084, and from Service Specifications 5.04 and 5.06 of the FY 88-89 Arizona Department of Corrections Service Specification Manual for additional reference. Some of the partial goals repeated below are from those documents.

a. To provide a coordinated institutional-community/reentry substance abuse intervention.

b. Interrupt progression towards substance use/abuse.

c. To decrease the use of or maintain abstinence from drugs/alcohol.

d. To improve emotional and mental well-being of the offender.

e. To provide for physical, emotional, religious, educational, and social needs of the offender.

f. To provide the environment to encourage responsibility, build self-esteem and self-reliance, develop work ethic, value authority, and take civic responsibility.

g. A comparison of the substance abuse model goals with the State program goals shows that there was good agreement on the desired outcome of this program.

# THE ULTIMATE GOAL – PROVIDE QUALITY CARE

In addition to the various technical goals set forth by the relevant funding and performing entities involved in this work, it was always important to maintain the focus of the special needs of the target population. Therefore, one unstated goal always took precedence above all others:

**Provide quality services and assurances consistent with the highest standards of professional mental health care delivery practices available.**

# GENERAL STRATEGY FOR ACHIEVING GOALS

With the large backdrop of goals and policies inherent to a major State contract of this nature, there was a need for a general program management approach to assure quality of care, and individual case success within the appropriate guidelines. That approach took the form of the following operating philosophy:

* Assess all cases for specific substance abuse treatment needs, and the individual's motivation and capacity to work towards change leading to successful balanced recovery and community reintegration.

* **Eclectically** serve each case by applying customized multimodal **treatment and coaching** tactics for addressing the specific need

areas unique to the individual, consistent with their motivation and capacity to work towards change.

*   As appropriate, apply the Esteem Therapy treatment methodology to general developmental and specific recovery need areas.

*   Manage all cases using Esteem Therapy as a strategic treatment plan focus, and for directing/implementing the application of eclectic tactics for change in those need areas where ET is not specifically used.

This comprehensive approach provided the means to satisfy the goals of delivering quality, need-fulfilling services, compliance with all State goals, and the opportunity for accumulation of statistically meaningful data for Esteem Therapy methodology over a wide range of environmental settings.

# Section A-IV

## *Service Delivery*

### Service Environment

### Institutional Locations

The Institutional Intervention segment of this work was provided in the following Arizona Department of Corrections juvenile institutions:

1. **Black Canyon Juvenile Institution** (BCJI) - A 120 secure bed correctional facility located in Maricopa County for **female** juvenile offenders between the ages of 8 through 17 who have been committed to the Arizona Department of Corrections. This facility provides diagnostic; reception; short, intermediate and long term treatment programming, as well as mental health programming.

During the period that this program was conducted, the cost for having each juvenile at this facility was $125.00/day, and the average length of confinement was 6 months. The general operating mode was for juveniles and security personnel to be uniformed, and a military school approach was typically used for escorted juvenile movements on the campus, and for designated activities.

2. **Adobe Mountain Juvenile Institution** (AMJI) - A 450 secure bed correctional facility located in Maricopa County for **male** juvenile offenders between the ages of 8 through 17 who have been committed to the Arizona Department of Corrections. This facility provides for the same general programming components as listed above for BCJI, plus some special components.

During the period this program was in effect, the cost for having each juvenile at this facility was $63.00/day, and the average length of confinement was 6 months. The general operating mode was for juveniles and security staff to be uniformed, but only mass population movements and certain designated activities were conducted using a military school approach.

At both of the juvenile facilities served during this program, all outside mental health care contract providers reported to the Psychologist II position of the Psychological Services department located at the facilities for clinical supervision, management, and coordination activities. As would be expected, certain interface operating problems were encountered by outside contractors providing mental health care services in these settings. A detailed discussion of those problems and solutions is beyond the scope of this report, however, the author may be contacted for detailed information.

# Community Locations

Community-based services were authorized to be provided at the following locations in Maricopa County during the contract period:

a. Provider's business location.

b. Department operated facilities, i.e. Desert Valley Learning Center, Ironwood, juvenile parole offices.

c. The offender's home.

d. Contracted residential treatment centers. One of these locations, i.e. Adventure Discovery, was in Coconino County, located in northern Arizona.

Of these potential locations, the offender's home resulted in being the most frequently used and successful for working with both the family and the juvenile on parole. From this provider's experience, home visits were the preferred location for community-based service delivery for various operational and therapeutic reasons. Since some of the population was from the lower economic class in the county, this activity often took place in welfare project housing neighborhoods and areas where drug sales and using activities were prevalent.

# SERVICE FORMATS AND POLICIES

## Institution

During the performance of this contract, services were provided in individual, group and family formats. Although the Institution Intervention phase utilized all three, individual sessions were most commonly used to accomplish the goals of treatment.

In addition to the normal direct contact formats used for communication with the juvenile in the institution, a special procedure was also established that allowed the person to make home telephone contact with the therapist under conditions of extreme stress, at the discretion of staff.

One of the primary purposes for using this approach was to teach the juvenile how to properly use the therapist as an important backup resource at times of perceived overwhelming crises. In practice this concept also helped to stabilize the institution when a juvenile had an affective management/control problem as a result of experiencing stressful/traumatic emotional feelings following intensive therapeutic work sessions. Considering the typical adversarial nature of the relationships between the juvenile and institution staff, this contact concept also served to provide a reality check for both parties and often resulted in defusing potentially volatile situations.

## Community

Service in the Community Support phase was provided in both individual and family formats. The structure of each session depended upon the needs of the individual and the family system at the time of the session. As previously mentioned, this work was performed in the home whenever possible to allow the provider to realistically assess the home and environmental dynamics, and to "join" the family system as both a **therapist and coach**. Operationally, this approach was also very successful for facilitating change in that system. In practice, it also eliminated the possibility of sabotage of the treatment continuum by either the individual or family due to schedule, or transportation problems/excuses.

When individual privacy was required with any member of the family during home visit sessions, an adequate location was always found either in the home, or outside. In many cases, individual sessions were conducted on the grounds of nearby city parks or schools that were within reasonable walking distance

To further improve the chances for program success with the individual and family in the community, services were also delivered on Saturdays, Sundays and holidays in those cases when the working parent(s) could not be available during the normal weekday. If the family was sincerely interested in supporting their child in their recovery program, this was accepted with good cooperation. Availability of the therapist on holidays was viewed by the family as dedicated behavior that underscored the importance of their child's recovery. In this situation, the therapist acted as a model to help the family members develop greater sensitivity and understanding. All of these "non-standard" home visit practices also reduced the frequency of family sabotage to service delivery.

Finally, as with the juvenile in the secure environment, the individual and family members were also provided with the therapist's home telephone number to allow appropriate contact under conditions of perceived crises, within limits defined by the therapist. It was experienced that limited, brief telephone contact under these conditions was successful. This mechanism provided realistic and therapeutic feedback for stabilizing the person, or family system until there could be direct contact. Feedback from the juvenile and family members was always positive regarding the availability of this aspect of service.

During the performance of this contract, and others over many years, this policy was never abused by a juvenile or family. Telephone calls were few, appropriate and always of short duration.

# SERVICE DELIVERY SCHEDULES

## Institutional Phase Duration Problem

The total length of service time available was not within the provider's control. The minimum length of institution confinement time that the juvenile could receive in Arizona was 3 months, but actual release was subject to institution board review, and was somewhat subject to treatment progress. From previous successful contract work using the Esteem Therapy substance abuse treatment model with this type of population at New Dawn Juvenile Institution (NDJI) in 1987, it was observed that 2-3 months of contact as a therapist and coach during the intervention phase in a controlled environment was very effective and often resulted in reduced substance abuse relapse and reduced institution recidivism rates.

Since the State purchasing agency planned to provide continued, long term support services in the community during the entire 6 month period the juvenile would be on parole, their initial general policy was to limit the

Institution Intervention phase to approximately 1 month. Additionally, it was learned that some juvniles referred to this program could be authorized to receive only the Institution Intervention services due to age, or geographical location upon release.

This policy appeared to be the result of the view by Purchase of Care that the contractor-provided institution intervention treatment service activities would have less impact on recovery than the community service component. The author disagreed with this policy and considered it a major potential obstacle to successful maintenance of the substance abuse recovery program based on the Esteem Therapy treatment model for the following reasons:

1. The severity and multi-dimensional nature of the underlying psychological stressors contributing to substance use/abuse requires intensive therapeutic work prior to the person's achievement of the behavioral changes, and development of the capacity to effectively support those changes for maintenance of a successful recovery program in the community.

An important premise in the Esteem Therapy substance abuse treatment model was that those issues would be sufficiently addressed. Historically, that work was observed to produce successful results when performed in a controlled environment.

2. The stresses and limitations of the controlled environment are advantageous and conducive for the precipitation of states of personal distress/trauma that allow in-depth focus on relevant developmental issues of affective management, deficient coping skills, trust, interpersonal relationships, and sensitive underlying psychological stressors.

In the Esteem Therapy model, formation of a special therapeutic relationship that emulates an ideal, effective parental matrix during these periods is important for correcting structural, as well as behavioral problems with this population. The opportunities for performing that level of work with this population are not normally available in the typical community setting where the influence of the real, dysfunctional parental matrix and dynamics exists and is operative.

3. The quality of the therapeutic relationship established in the limited institutional environment facilitates the means for the juvenile's learning effective utilization of the Esteem therapist as a predictable resource, coach and trusted source of reality feedback once in the community.

4. Behavioral regression during treatment in the institution can be successfully analyzed and used therapeutically for working on the individual's substance use relapse dynamics with less risk of exposure and/or access to dangerous substances. (Scannell, J. (1988). "Esteem Therapy: A New Treatment Approach For Recovering populations." Paper presented at Arizona Department of Corrections training seminar on 4/4/88 in Phoenix, Arizona.)

The Esteem Therapy substance abuse treatment model applies the concept of a "prolapse" as an experience that presents an important opportunity for learning. The subsequent prolapse analysis can be much more instructive and productive when it takes place in a safe, controlled environment compared to a community setting.

As a result of the serious program concerns associated with these issues, a theoretically viable alternative approach was devised to provide a new, yet practical solution for those juveniles receiving reduced Institution Intervention service time.

# Variable Service Delivery Rate Concept

The solution conceived was based on the observation that the state purchasing agency did not impose constraints on the maximum number of sessions, session frequency, or session length used to deliver services in this program. Therefore, services could legitimately be provided using a variable service delivery rate and schedule approach for the sessions.

When applying the Esteem Therapy substance abuse treatment model in previous contract activities with this same type of population and setting, it had been observed that frequency and time were session variables that could be successfully controlled and altered to produce therapeutic progress that ranged from comparable to accelerated, when compared with the standard (and expected) 1-hour/week session schedule. Therefore, when insufficient Institution Intervention Phase time became an important issue regarding case progress prior to release, session frequency-time schedule modifications were implemented to compensate for reduced service duration. In practice this often resulted in conducting up to three1- hour sessions/week.

For difficult cases that were recognized by staff as particularly compatible with the Esteem Therapy substance abuse model, but where the intervention treatment time scheduled by Purchase of Care for institution services was severely limited, total service time was often increased at the **direct request of institution staff**.

In addition to exercising the option for increasing the time of sessions as required to compensate for reduced total service duration, the general delivery approach applied for conducting all sessions was to utilize whatever length of time was necessary for accomplishing the therapeutic goals. This was consistent with the conviction that the program must always respond to the unique treatment needs of the person with the appropriate quality of care, as stated in the goals section of this report.

Although a standard one hour session was often "allotted" prior to individual sessions, the resulting depth and intensity of emotions uncovered during sessions that addressed underlying stressors such as sexual abuse, family dysfunction, and guilt/shame and some developmental issues generally required 1.5 - 2.0 hours for acceptable therapeutic processing and closure. Similarly, difficult behavioral issues such as depression, suicidal ideation, sexual identity and relationship conflicts also typically required more than the standard 1 hour session time for successful resolution.

## Institution Family Service Delivery

During the same treatment time period available in the institution for the individual, family services were also to be initiated approximately two weeks prior to the juvenile's planned release. Since this activity was limited by Purchase of Care to only 2 sessions prior to the completion of the Institution Intervention phase, the therapeutic productivity associated with this activity was similarly limited. In practice, little could realistically be accomplished beyond rapport building and preliminary coaching, an introduction to the services, rules negotiations, and how the therapist would serve as a support for the juvenile and family in the community. The concept of the therapist's role as a link in the continuum of services available was also discussed.

Although an unlimited session time approach was also used to attempt to compensate for the reduced number of sessions in the institution, they rarely exceeded 2 hours in length because of the time constraints of the parents. Often, these sessions had to be scheduled for a Saturday or Sunday during the visiting hour times allowed by the institution.

## Community Service Delivery

Although one session each week was often adequate for family services in the community, some were serviced several times each week on an as-needed basis due to the unique treatment problems and needs. This was especially true when self-destructive behaviors, such as substance relapse or suicidal ideation were recognized as probable choices for the recovering person.

Institution family session lengths were easier to control and conduct successfully within a standard 1.5 hour time frame when that was necessary, however, community family work often depended upon many conditions. It was observed that members typically saved serious conflicts and problem solving issues until the therapist was present. The community family sessions often required 2 - 2.5 hours of time.

# SERVICE DOCUMENTATION

Various session and program-related documentation was prepared and submitted on a regular basis. Two forms were produced by the provider by printing relevant program information onto existing State form 50000031, Rev. 1/30/89. The purpose of this overprint was to add significant information for accurate tracking of treatment phase and to support the quantitative collection goals of the application of the Esteem Therapy substance abuse model. Copies of all forms can be provided by the author upon request. A brief description of each form is given below.

## Session Chronological Form

This form was a 3-part chronological case report document, prepared immediately following each session. In addition to the normal juvenile and therapist identification data that was entered, the therapist also noted the phase of treatment addressed during the session, and the primary treatment methodology applied. Observations and comments were then made regarding the therapeutic work and other relevant issues. Finally, session progress and future plans were noted. To complete this form, the date session length, session type and session location were then added. When this form was completed, 1 copy/part was retained in the provider's records and the remaining 2 parts were submitted to the State juvenile records department in the institution for filing.

## Final Service Treatment Plan Summary

This 3-part treatment termination form was also produced by the provider by printing over the same existing State form as used for the chronological documentation. This form included the same identifying data, primary treatment methodology, reason for the termination of treatment services, progress towards satisfying the Service Treatment plan, and final recommendations. When completed, one copy/part of this form was retained in the provider's records and the remaining 2 parts were submitted to the State juvenile records department in the institution for filing.

## Monthly Progress Report

The Substance Abuse Services Monthly Progress Report forms were produced by the State purchasing agency for use by providers. This form was completed at the end of each month and functioned as a record of services provided during that month in support of invoices submitted for compensation. In addition to indicating pertinent treatment plan progress, it was necessary to list the methodologies applied. This documentation also supported formal tracking of the use of the Esteem Therapy substance abuse model. This completed form was submitted along with monthly invoices to the Purchase of Care unit of the Arizona Department of Corrections. The provider also retained a copy in each juvenile's records. A copy of the front side of this report is provided in this report as Figures A-X-10.

## Substance Abuse Treatment Plan

Figures A-VII-1, A-VII-2 and A-VII-3 are copies of special visual aids that served an important part of the ET treatment plan. These basic documents, developed by the provider, were specifically related to the treatment plan used during this program. Generally, the treatment plan was developed by the third session and placed in the juvenile's file on the same day. Since the planning process, visual aids and documentation are discussed in detail in the section that addresses treatment planning they will not be described here.

# Section A-V

## *The Population Served*

### POPULATION DESCRIPTION

### General Description – Maricopa County Juvenile Court Center Survey

A 1990 survey of children committed to the state Department of Corrections was prepared by the Maricopa County Juvenile Court Center, Research and Planning Department, to provide a general description of the 600 children from Maricopa County committed to the Arizona Department of Corrections in 1989. This figure represents 70 percent of all the children committed in the State of Arizona.

Since the vast majority of the children treated in this contract were from Maricopa County, some of the descriptive information learned in this survey, that also applies to the 108 cases served during this program, is repeated here as a summary.

* Average age at commitment was 15½ and almost 9 out of 10 were boys.

* 40 percent were committed for property crimes such as car theft, 18 percent for violent offenses and 26 percent for "obstruction" offenses such as resisting arrest, running away or violating probation.

* Youths committed to the Department of Corrections had committed an average of more than 4 offenses previously.

* 1/2 of those committed were Anglo, half minorities.

* More than 1/3 had failed at least one grade, and most were not attending school when committed.

* More than 1/2 came from dysfunctional homes, and 1/3 had been abused.

* 2/3 of the adolescent males and 1/2 of the adolescent females had trouble controlling their anger.

* 35 percent of the adolescent females and 17 percent of the adolescent males had been hospitalized for emotional problems. 14 percent had attempted suicide.

* 1 out of 10 adolescent males indicated they had been sexually abused or had sexually abused others.

* 9 out of 10 had drug or alcohol problems.

Direct treatment experience during this contract and previous contract activities with this population generally confirmed the above results provided in this survey. However, as a result of more detailed knowledge and analyses of the 108 cases served, some quantitative deviations were discovered when comparing several areas of the survey with the large number of cases treated. Therefore, those survey areas were omitted from the above and will be presented in the information given below.

# The Population Treated in this Program

The following summary specifically describes the 108 case population treated during this program, and is the result of analysis of some of the raw data shown in Tables I and II of Appendix A-X.

* 14 percent of the population had serious psychological problems.

* 97 percent of the population were from dysfunctional family systems.

* 99 percent of the population had serious self-esteem problems.

* 90 percent of the female population were either confirmed, or highly probable to have been sexually abused.

* 62 percent of the population had a history of abusing more than 2 different substances.

* 76 percent of the population had an alcohol abuse problem.

If a similar summary were made up to describe the parents of this population, much of the same information revealed in the above studies for the children would be expected to also apply, especially in the areas of family dysfunction, substance abuse and sexual/physical abuse.

# POPULATION REFERRAL PROCESS

## General Selection Information

**No exclusionary criteria** was sought or imposed in this contract because the most random, unbiased assignments possible were desired for meaningful model verification. Because of previous success and experience with "hard core" chemically dependent adolescent females, however, the majority of the referrals received were primarily of that type. Of the 108 cases, only 15 were males. As a result, most of the institution Intervention work was accomplished at the new Black Canyon Juvenile Institution (BCJI) for females. This facility formerly initiated full operational status on November 1, 1988.

## The Referral Process

Prior to the State's universal implementation of a formal referral process, all referrals received by this provider were initiated by either the assigned institution case worker, or clinical psychologist following the diagnostic assessment process in the institution. At the time of the inception of this contract, female offenders were still being served under an existing substance abuse treatment contract at both New Dawn Juvenile Institution (NDJI) and Alamo Juvenile Institution (AJI) on the basis of the institution referral procedure only.

The official document used for authorizing and controlling the referral of offenders to the substance abuse treatment program, initiated several months later, was the Arizona Department of Corrections **Youth Parole Plan (YPP)**. This form was initiated by the youth's Parole Officer (PO) as developed from various file data, interviews and institution diagnostic assessment tools. In addition to relevant descriptive information concerning the youth/family, and recommended parole conditions, the form also contained a "needs" section that included the categories of psychiatric, substance abuse, educational, emotional/behavioral, independent living and vocational needs for that particular individual.

The choices available to the PO for indicating those needs were limited to High (H), Medium (M), and Low (L). Those substance abuse needs designated as "H" were viewed as chemically dependent/abusive; medium corresponded to heavy, or "at risk" users; and low were either viewed as experimental users, or undetermined.

From November 1, 1988 to April 1, 1989, a combination of the two procedures was in effect. Therefore, some of the cases reported in Table 1 of Appendix A-X had been originally referred by case workers or psychologists, and the formal YPP authorization form for the Institution Intervention phase of treatment did not yet exist. Once the YPP procedure was refined, all referrals were received by the provider via delivery by the U.S. Postal Service

## Referral Verification – Screening

As previously noted, the YPP form contained the first official substance abuse information regarding a new referral that was made available to the provider. Occasionally the form was received with a packet of file data that contained important historical background information, however, this was the exception rather than the rule. Since a validated substance abuse screening instrument for assessment and evaluation was not available from the State during the time this contract was performed, this provider assessed the substance abuse treatment needs and program appropriateness of each person on the basis of four different source modes of discovery for accurate assessment, as needed. Those modes were:

A. File data.
B. Clinical interview sessions.
C. Written Narcotics Anonymous/Alcoholics Anonymous 1st Step documentation (modified).
D. Feedback from family and significant peers.

As a result of using these sources in different combinations during the first several sessions, more extensive lifestyle substance-use information was always acquired than was originally available in the individual's file, or any other single location. In almost all instances it was discovered that the reported substance abuse problems had been minimized and were far more severe than the file indicated. **As seen in Table I, of the 108 cases served in this program, 1 was "L", 12 were "M" and the remaining 95 cases were listed as belonging in the "H" category of substance abuse treatment needs.** Using the combination methodology developed for population assessment/screening, these assignments were verified.

As previously noted, most of the cases referred to this provider were typically considered "hard core" by both the community and the Arizona Department of Corrections. Therefore, an "H" designation was also normally indicated for the areas of psychiatric and emotional/behavioral needs. These needs were easily confirmed during the clinical interview, as well as from the information contained in the file.

The written Narcotics Anonymous/Alcoholics Anonymous (N.A./A.A.) First Step activity was not used for all cases, but in those instances where it was applied, it was very successful as both a self-reporting and therapeutic instrument. This approach revealed an in-depth view of the lifestyle pervasiveness of the substance abuse problem, and also permitted valuable intimate therapeutic contact to be made early as a result of the traumatic emotional content associated with the information disclosed. Completion of that activity required "homework" for the juvenile and one long individual session with the therapist to process the sensitive oral presentation. The original document was retained in the provider's file to confront denial if it occurred in the future.

These early assessment/screening process activities for verifying program appropriateness and needs were a very important part of the intervention treatment phase of the program because it facilitated formation of the effective therapeutic matrix/alliance while providing valuable historical knowledge.

# Section A-VI:

## *Treatment Services*

### GENERAL TREATMENT SERVICES

### Treatment Management Strategy

As indicated in the Program Goals section, Section A-III, the treatment strategy was always customized to best satisfy the person's needs using the highest quality of care service possible. From that perspective, the **Esteem Therapy** model acknowledged and respected each individual's uniqueness in terms of treatment and capacity for change leading to a personal recovery program.

An important operational outcome of this approach was the management of each case using **Esteem Therapy as a general therapeutic and coaching framework** for overall treatment focus and direction, while utilizing all other available therapeutic techniques in a multi-modal, eclectic manner to facilitate the recovery process. Since this process depended upon the successful use of different methods at different times, a single "canned" program for universal application to all cases cannot be described. Instead, the various methodologies used successfully during different phases and stages of the substance abuse treatment program is discussed below.

# General Institution Intervention Phase Services

As emphasized in Section A-IV regarding service delivery, taking advantage of the unique opportunity for success that was available and could be realized during this phase of treatment was viewed as vital for both interrupting and redirecting the self-destructive path that the juvenile had been following until this point of intervention. Inasmuch as the referrals treated in this program would receive and utilize community services over a wide range, this provider considered it essential that the total population be given sufficient institution intervention phase services to maintain the change in path direction once interrupted and redirected, regardless of the level of community support services. For example, some referrals would not be authorized to receive any services, while others authorized to receive it may not have had the capacity to effectively use it once returned to their dysfunctional, non-supportive family system.

From previous experience, both types of cases can be given adequate therapy, knowledge and coping resources and coaching to maintain an improved functioning lifestyle and recovery from self-destructive behaviors, including substance abuse without regular professional support services. To accomplish that goal during this contract, critical Institution Intervention phase treatment services were delivered in the following general stages.

I.   Assessment/Screening.

II.  Treatment Planning.

III. Intervention Treatment.

IV.  Family/Community Transition Planning.

V.   Family Treatment.

VI.  Institution Termination.

An outline listing the different treatment methodologies and the purposes for which they were most often used at each of these stages is provided later in this section. From this outline, it is obvious that a wide variety of methodologies were used, as necessary, for treatment at different stages of the intervention phase. For the juvenile, as well as the family, those selected for use at any given point in time was a function of their needs and capacity to work at that point.

Of the various treatment issues referred to in the outline and focused on throughout this phase, several are noteworthy for discussion because they were significant for resolution in terms of both generalized self-esteem recovery and development, and recovery from substance abuse. Two of those issues are connoted in the terms "Emotional processing" and "Victim Abuse Processing and Treatment".

# Emotional Processing

The presence of the Emotional processing component shown under the Esteem Therapy methodology at various locations in the outline is a direct reflection of the pivotal importance attached to treatment of the special emotional needs of this population. As noted in describing the general population, and verified on a case-by-case basis during clinical interviews, a high percentage of these children experienced a serious pattern of abandonment, neglect, deprivation and/or abusive treatment from their dysfunctional family of origin. These patterns contribute to the formation of serious structural self-esteem defects and painful underlying stressors.

It was hypothesized in the Esteem Therapy substance abuse treatment model that:

**The addition of negative lifestyle effects from substance use/abuse to this damaging family background during the child's developmental stages can significantly influence the formation of a distorted and dysfunctional self structure.**

As distorted and dysfunctional as this structure may appear to the outside world, however, for all intents and purposes, it was often perceived by the juvenile as both need fulfilling and functional. Indeed, given their family system of origin and the history of abusive treatment, it certainly may feel more functional than what they experienced in the home. To escape, or even achieve some temporary relief from the constant underlying painful feelings caused by those negative and esteem-damaging experiences, substance use/ abuse makes perfect sense to the person if that is the only behavior choice that has worked so far.

Some typical substance use/abuse related issues that are addressed by the emotional processing therapeutic component in all sessions include the following:

1. Grief issues.
2. Age/role-appropriate emotions and confusion.
3. Emotional inhibition and regression.

4. Family dysfunction.

5. Co-dependency issues.

The significant success of the ET-based treatment regime for persons having these underlying problems was partly due to the in-depth appreciation of the emotional causes and effects leading to that scenario, and the immediate experience of relief and hope that results from the feeling that **someone finally understands and can help,** without allowing the child's problematic behavior to get in the way.

Although some special ET techniques were required for effectively engaging the person at this level during the first meeting/assessment session, the dramatic success of ET was often simply due to the early initiation of empathic processing of those sensitive issues with care and respect for the person's choice of pace and often limited capacity to work at intensive levels. This was typically accomplished to the point that some relief from the psychological and emotional pain related to those issues was normally experienced and commented on by the juvenile by the end of that session. Additionally, when the therapist acts in the role of a **"coach,"** the process is perceived as a team effort that has more capacity then the individual striving alone for achieving change.

Because that person successfully experienced and, therefore, associated some relief from painful underlying feelings while working with the Esteem Therapist, this was one of the most important ways that the therapeutic/coaching relationship quickly became need-fulfilling for facilitating the creation of the motivational state desired for them to commit to enter the treatment program. Additionally, it is highly probable that, for the very first time in that person's life, they perceived that there was reason for hope in learning to relieve their emotional pain, and feel better about themselves without the use of drugs or alcohol.

The therapist's processing of this experience also supports the contention that the important motivational state for change was then created, and needed only to be encouraged through appropriate coaching for sustenance. It is important to point out that if creation of the motivational state to change was accomplished and could be sustained from session to session, then the important treatment model goal for early development and maintenance of their minimum level of self-esteem was, in fact, accomplished at this initial stage.

# Victim Abuse Processing and Treatment

The victim Abuse Processing component also listed in various locations in the Institution Intervention phase primarily refers to addressing the female sexual abuse issues. As noted in the population description summary in Section A-V, 90 percent of the total female population served had either confirmed, or was considered probable as having experienced sexual abuse. In many of these cases, the abuse was not a single event, but a series of events that took place over a period of months, or even years within the same family system. Furthermore, if they hadn't

experienced sexual abuse in the family system, but had a history of running away from home and living on the "street," then sexually exploitation by drug suppliers and others certainly was common during those times.

Although the primary focus of this program was to treat the juvenile offenders for substance abuse, the presence of various serious abuse experiences, such as sexual and physical abuse, in nearly every case required intensive treatment in those areas as a matter of course for general self-esteem recovery, as well as recovery from substance abuse. With the exception of the structural impact that the general pattern of long term abuse, neglect and deprivation from family caretakers had on the development of the self, sexual abuse of the female juvenile was considered by the provider to be the single, most significant underlying **psychological stressor** and probable contributing causative factor for substance abuse to be resolved for successful recovery, especially "balanced" recovery.

This activity was performed utilizing the ET victim abuse treatment model in conjunction with the Emotional processing component. Although the details of this work will not be discussed in this special report, some of the specific primary sex abuse victim impact issues addressed during the Institution Intervention Phase of treatment is described below. These emotional and developmental issues have also been duly noted as significant for resolution by other experienced workers in the field of victim abuse recovery.

1. Low self-esteem, and accompanying deficiencies in the perception of self.
2. Loss of self-mastery/control, or personal power.
3. Reduced ability to trust in relationships.
4. Repressed anger and hostility.
5. Depression.
6. Guilt.
7. Fear.
8. Blurred role boundaries and role confusion.
9. "Damaged Goods" syndrome.

10. Sexual identity confusion.

11. Pseudo-maturity, coupled with the failure to accomplish the developmental tasks normal for their level.

12. Abandonment by family and society as "throw-aways."

Obviously, some of the above issues were also generally present with this population as a result of other factors, but where they were the specific outcome of an identified series of traumatic events, they required unique treatment attention for successful resolution.

The Esteem Therapy victim abuse treatment model proved to be very successful with such cases because of the special focus on self-esteem and the importance of personal **empowerment** in both treatment and long-term recovery. The use of techniques for re-empowering the person in treatment began long before sexual abuse was addressed on an intensive basis. Therefore, by the time some individuals were ready to work with their abuse issues, they had already achieved an improved sense of personal power and higher self-esteem in their lives.

The special trusting therapeutic relationship established with the esteem therapist facilitated working at intensive levels for successful resolution of those sensitive and difficult problem areas. As with the issues that were related to the other forms of emotional processing, the earlier that progress was made, the better in terms of development and maintenance of the minimum level of self-esteem for the substance abuse and other recovery work still to be accomplished. Since this issue represented one of the key underlying psychological stressors when it present, the first breakthrough towards creation of the motivational state for change often occurred simultaneously with progress in that area.

# Reactions to Treatment

For the intensive therapeutic work performed in the juvenile institutions served during this contract, as well as previous contracts, it was consistently observed for those areas addressed by emotional processing and victim abuse processing, that treatment progress was usually accompanied by notable behavioral and/or physical reactions. Given the highly traumatic nature of the content and the very likely probability of releasing repressed/suppressed feelings, this was not an unexpected phenomenon.

In most cases, the behavioral reactions were simply the result of a need for additional emotional processing through some physical means. Sensitive case workers and unit staff, especially those at BCJI, were usually able to cope with occasional acting-out behaviors, and support the juvenile in their efforts for that release when they had some warning that the person might react in that way.

Physical reactions/symptoms, such as vomiting, high fevers, etc. were more subtle, and unfortunately not as easy to recognize and deal with by institution staff. For those manifestations, the therapist generally must be available for continuity and resolution. Use of the special home telephone communications format offered by the provider for maintaining the required therapeutic continuity was very successful in facilitating resolution and stability for the person (and the institution) in both of these areas when treatment reaction occurred. Additionally, the frequent application of recreational therapy techniques and dream analysis/processing during subsequent session work was often successful in reducing, or interrupting the effects of physical reactions.

# GENERAL COMMUNITY SUPPORT SERVICES

This phase contained the treatment services delivered in the community in support of both the juvenile and the family. Some of the major tasks required of the therapist/coach during this part of the program included the following:

1. Effectively treat/support the juvenile and family/community for successful reintegration.

2. Facilitate the family/community efforts in supporting the juvenile for successful maintenance of their substance abuse recovery program. This included training the parents in the use of improved **parenting and coaching techniques**.

3. Facilitate the family/community efforts in supporting the juvenile for successful compliance with their State of Arizona Youth Parole Plan (YPP).

4. Continuation of relevant intervention treatment plan goals for successful resolution.

5. Ongoing assessment and monitoring.

6. Coordination of treatment with residential staff, if at placement.

7. Coordination with the Parole Officer (PO).

8. Coordination with educators in the school system.

9. Coordination with State employment support personnel

10. General linkage with all other treatment services available in the continuum.

A brief outline of the stages and general treatment methodologies applied for effectively accomplishing the above tasks during this phase is listed below.

I.    Family/community Assessment and Reintegration Stage.
    A.  Esteem Therapy
    B.  Cognitive Therapy
    C.  Reality Therapy
    D.  Education Therapy

II. Family/community Treatment and Support Stage.
    A.  Esteem Therapy
    B.  Cognitive Therapy
    C.  Reality Therapy
    D.  Education Therapy
    E.  Recreation Therapy
    F.   Parenting Information
    G.  Coaching Techniques

III. Family/community Aftercare Stage
    A.  Esteem Therapy
    B.  Cognitive Therapy
    C.  Parenting Information
    D.  Coaching Techniques

IV. Family/community Termination Stage
    A.  Esteem Therapy
    B.  Cognitive Therapy
    C.  Education Therapy

As with the Institution Intervention phase, Esteem Therapy was the overall treatment management strategy. Methods from many other methodologies were applied as needed, and used in conjunction with ET.

# General Family Treatment Issues

The community support services provided to the family members often addressed issues that were enabling the juvenile's substance abuse, behavioral patterns, such as their own dysfunctional behaviors, including substance abuse, co-dependency, etc. As possible, a recovery program for them was developed. The details concerning that information are beyond the scope of this document.

# Section A-VII

## *Specific Intervention Treatment Techniques*

Although the multimodal treatment delivery approach was important for providing the variety of services required to meet the special recovery needs of each person, some of the techniques used in this program were unique to the **Esteem Therapy** model, and particularly noteworthy for producing successful results with nearly all children and young adults. Although a detailed presentation of these techniques cannot be provided in this limited report, a brief introduction and discussion of some of these methods is given below.

## ESTEEM THERAPY

Esteem Therapy was used throughout the program, first as the case management and focusing strategy and secondly, as applicable, for addressing specific treatment issues, such as self-esteem. Since the case management and focusing strategy aspects have been addressed during the discussion of general institution treatment services, this section will focus on specific techniques that were successful in that phase. The three intervention phase areas in which ET techniques have been observed to make a significant impact towards facilitating change in the person were the **Assessment/Screening**, **Treatment Planning**, and **Treatment** stages.

# ET Assessment/Screening Stage Techniques

A basic ET substance abuse model premise was that the person whose path has been interrupted must initially be motivated to work towards change before any formal path of recovery can be embarked upon. The success of the esteem therapist in that area has often been dramatic. Beginning with the introduction to the therapist, the relationship was carefully crafted for the juvenile to experience feelings of value as a person, **unconditionally**, regardless of what their behaviors may have been prior to their arrival at this point in their life.

Motivation for entering and engaging in the recovery program starting with the assessment stage and continuing throughout the total treatment program was the result of the development and maintenance of a sufficiently **need-fulfilling** relationship. In addition to valuing the person, regardless of behaviors, other therapeutic characteristics that were vital for success in this area included the perception that the therapist was caring, competent and consistent, especially in terms of their respect for the person's right to make choices.

Nearly simultaneous with the important development of that motivation was the experience of therapeutic engagement that confers feelings of empowerment as a member of a **team** that has the capacity and competency for recovery, if they choose to commit to that path. In this capacity, the therapist is perceived as a **coach** that will unwaveringly accompany the person on their path for recovery.

Once the person appreciated the fact that they would be valued as a person by the therapist/coach **regardless of their choice**, the important psychological bridge for commitment and change was established. It was made clear that should they **choose** to participate in a substance abuse treatment program for recovery they would have increased personal power and competent support. Therefore, the first ET-related treatment issue to be addressed was that of the choice to engage in treatment, or not. The therapist acting as a coach facilitated this decision-making process by emphasizing the team approach for the effort. It should be mentioned that the person's decision to participate in this program also meant that they would be **solely responsible** for their progress and success, not the therapist/coach. Thus, they would **"own"** the choice and results.

Empowerment for change beginning with the assessment stage and continuing throughout the treatment process was accomplished using a variety of ET techniques that always focused on the concept of personal choice/self-determination consistent with the esteeming and supportive aspects of the therapeutic/coaching relationship. Developed and maintained in the correct manner, the operational matrix represented and used by that relationship functioned in much the same way as the ideal effective parental matrix for the developing child.

# ET Treatment Planning Stage Techniques

Following the general Assessment/Screening stage, further expansion of the sense of empowerment was specifically accomplished through the completion of activities that were designed to focus on **choice and teamwork** during the Intervention Treatment Planning Stage. The planning activity was specifically developed using ET to engage, enjoin and support the person in the process of change, and communicate/teach some of the general principles of recovery and the prevention of relapse. This activity was performed using a 2-stage approach that typically required 2 separate individual sessions.

The first session presented the general recovery strategy in the form of a journey metaphor for visually communicating significant elements of their general plan for change. This technique used a mountain hiking path metaphor that included the use of a map for following what was referred to as the "**Path of Recovery**."

The second session presented the formal treatment plan document that was consistent with the map, but allowed the person to identify specific changes that all agree should be made for them to successfully travel and **stay** on the path. While it was important for the person to know that the therapist would accompany them on their journey as a coach and member of the team, the concepts of **responsibility and ownership** of both the problems and the plan for change and recovery was inherent to their participation during these two stages. Some of the information associated with the completion of these two stages is discussed below.

# Path of Recovery Map

Figure A-VII-1, shown below, is a reduced size photocopy of the Path of Recovery metaphor map used prior to the development of the formal treatment plan. A full scale copy of the map used as a worksheet in this session can be provided by email from the author upon request.

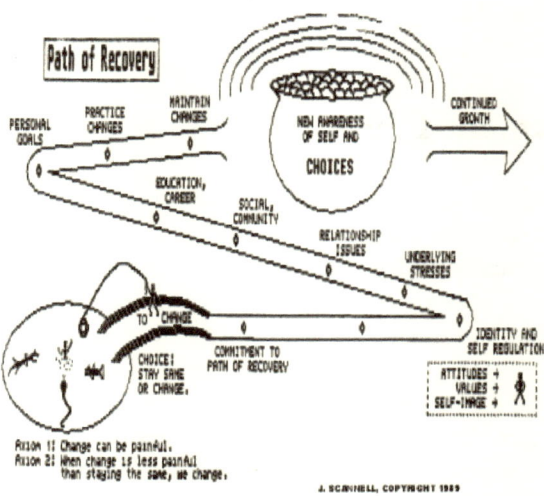

**Figure A-VII-1. Photocopy of Path of Recovery map/worksheet used in treatment planning and treatment. (70% reduction)**

This computer-generated map was typically explained and given to the juvenile in the second or third session of treatment. Since this was an interactive task, this session normally required 1.5 - 2 hours of time for successful completion.

The comments and questions used by the therapist, acting as the coach during this presentation, were especially designed and **scripted** to communicate certain information that was important to be understood and eventually internalized. A general description of the verbiage and approach required for correctly working through this task is included in this report, however, additional information can be provided upon request.

During this process, specific comparisons were made between hiking up a steep mountain trail and following the steep path of recovery from self-destructive behaviors, such as substance abuse. In particular, it was called to the person's attention that **choice** was at the crux of the issue for entering treatment, maintaining recovery, and for the behaviors used if a slip/lapse occurred during the process.

While it was made clear that the final responsibility for change and staying on the path belonged to the individual, it was important for them to understand that caring, competent support would be available and may be necessary from time-to-time, especially during difficult parts of the climb, or when slips occur. This concept allowed the therapist to join the person as a **coach** on their path as the member of the team having special skills and support for recovery.

At the completion of this activity, the person's name was written on the map and it was given to them to take to their living unit for tracking purposes. An important aspect of their having the map in their possession was that it represented a concrete form of **"ownership"** for their program and commitment for change. Some of them had it laminated and put on their bookcase for easy reference and discussion with others. In nearly all cases, they proudly showed this map and their progress to their families.

# FORMAL TREATMENT PLAN

The formal Intervention Treatment Plan document consisted of 2 pages developed during a separate session following the session with the presentation of the map. This plan essentially tracked the map, but also contained some unique subtleties that were consistent with various aspects of their recovery, including principles of ET, the substance abuse treatment model, and the prevention of relapse to substance abuse. It was also important to note that the role of choice throughout this activity continued to be emphasized. A copy of this plan can be provided by email from the author upon request.

**Goal A** of the plan was stated as follows: ***Commit to making the changes needed to travel on the path of recovery from past behaviors or events.***

This first goal was typically accomplished prior to this formal session, therefore, the juvenile had already experienced success in treatment. If the map were present at this session, the first open diamond-shaped symbol at the beginning of the path could be colored in solid. Generally, that was done during the map session. It should be noted here that the interesting parallels that Goal A has to the N.A./A.A. 1st Step approach were by design, and not by accident.

**Goal B** - ***Identify what is to be changed to travel and stay on the path*** of the treatment plan. – This was the goal that allowed the person to actively participate in identifying and negotiating what was to be worked on, but could also be useful in removing residual resistance/denial of problems in specific areas. Since this was the first goal that focused on, and documented the stressful problems to be acknowledged in different areas, the Esteem Therapist was often confrontational in filling out this part of the plan. Reality Therapy (RT) methods used in conjunction with ET were successful for that purpose.

When working with this part of the plan, only very short comments or key words were necessary or desirable for entry in the available spaces. Since a copy of this plan was to be placed in the person's Department of Corrections file, this approach was also valued by the person because it conveyed the importance of protecting their confidentiality.

Ideally, the second goal was completed by the end of the 3rd session, but the therapist filled in the actual session in which completion occurs, thereby acting as a role model with regard to goal targets and schedules for completion. If the person was actively tracking their treatment progress using the map shown in Figure A-VII-1, they were encouraged to fill in the appropriate diamond-shaped symbols on their own.

**Goal C** - *Develop, practice and maintain the means for change, or resolution*. This goal was similar to Goal A in the sense that it was meant to communicate/educate regarding the process of change, and that that **process was ongoing**. It should be noted that Goal C was linked conceptually to the continued growth that is implied at the top of the hiking path map, and to the philosophy of recovery from addictive behaviors. Since it was open-ended and ongoing, the person is told that parts of the plan would continue with the therapist if they receive community support services. Otherwise, they would be responsible for continuing their plan to stay in recovery. In any case, it was important that they understood that they would not be kept in the institution longer due to this goal being incomplete.

The second page of this plan consisted of the development of specific goals with realistic target dates. This was very important from the viewpoint of Esteem Therapy, and was designed to allow for the coached, guided development of individual, need-fulfilling goals that the person **wanted** to achieve, and essentially had total control over. These goals may not have coincided with the goals of therapy, goals of the facility, goals of the State, or any other goals in which someone else had a stake regarding the completion or outcome.

The juvenile was encouraged and assisted in developing appropriate personal goals during this stage of treatment for the following reasons:

1. To begin to re-empower, or newly empower the person outside of the therapeutic relationship.

2. To provide the opportunity to experience the feelings of personal control in at least **one** part of their life over which they should have power.

3. To teach the important elements in the process of successful goal setting regarding reality, practicality, timing and flexibility.

4. To teach the power of goal setting for achieving wants/needs.

5. To provide concrete demonstration/proof of respect for their choices.

6. To provide the opportunity to experience feelings of personal competency and worth, if goal achievement is successful. Although this is early in the Intervention Phase of treatment, this task established

the important first building block leading to the development of new self-esteem from the minimum level.

7. To provide the opportunity to experience the feelings of non-critical support, and acquire the capability for re-planning to realistically achieve goals, if unsuccessful.

8. To provide the opportunity for identifying self-defeating behavior patterns if unsuccessful for that reason.

In practice, the goal development task was accomplished with the therapist acting as the **coach** and scribe while guiding the person through the various written parts of the goals. Generally, this was a new experience for the juvenile, so they often required some prompting and the therapist's/coach's assistance in defining the goals, and methods for achieving the goals.

Typical personal goals for the female offenders have been to stop biting nails, lose weight, make friends, etc. In addition, however, they often selected therapeutic treatment-related goals, such as to improve assertive communication skills, improve relationship with family members, etc. Although only two goals of this nature were generally developed at this time, they were encouraged to add more on their own in the future, and some were successful in that effort.

When the total plan was completed, the second page was signed and dated by both therapist and juvenile. The original and one copy of this document was forwarded to their permanent Department of Corrections file, one copy was retained by the therapist, and a copy was given to the juvenile for their use and reference.

Feedback from the individual and staff regarding this planning activity was very positive and often enthusiastic because of the progress made. Although the map and formal plan each required from 1.5 - 2.0 hours of session time, these activities had significant therapeutic impact due to their emphasis on motivation, empowerment and insight. Additionally, the juvenile left these sessions with something tangible to access for tracking their own treatment progress, and for institution presentation occasions, such as review/release boards, staffing, etc. when they were likely to be questioned regarding their work in the substance abuse treatment area. Similarly, it was also learned that the juvenile often shared the map and substance abuse treatment progress information with parents and others during visitations.

# ET TREATMENT STAGE TECHNIQUES

Esteem Therapy was also very successful in addressing specific need areas during the formal treatment stage of the Intervention Phase of the institution program services. Although it was important to continually monitor the person throughout the total treatment process regarding motivation and empowerment, it was observed that the operational consistency provided in the therapeutic and coaching relationship was sufficient to maintain those benefits while facilitating the goals for change in the identified areas, and the development of higher levels of self-esteem.

During the formal Institution Intervention Treatment Stage, several unique ET techniques were successful for accomplishing the goals of the treatment model. For brevity in this report, only the one considered to have had the most significant and enduring impact on long term recovery and stability will be discussed. That was the activity known as the **Developmental Pyramid**.

# The Developmental Pyramid

The identified areas for change, as jointly determined during the write-up of Goal B in the treatment plan, addressed significant and current practical problems for the juvenile in all of the normal and developmental areas of their life, including **identity, relationships and dealing with the world**. Since neither the need nor the means for change in these areas were well understood by the recovering person at that time, the additional motivation necessary to do the hard work usually associated with that stage of treatment was lacking.

It was found that the person in treatment had improved understanding and motivation regarding the need and means for change in those areas when they were discussed in terms of the same general categories/dimensions of **behavioral/personal, relational** and **reality** that have been used to the explain the development of the self in the Pyramid Model. Because that model provided the theoretical basis for Esteem Therapy, the introduction and use of certain information from the Developmental Pyramid Model at that critical juncture was also considered an important foundation step towards the future correction of structural self-esteem defects, and growth of new, higher levels of self-esteem.

Figure A-VII-2 shown below is a reduced size photocopy of the basic Pyramid Model used with the person during the treatment stage of the Intervention Phase. A full scale copy of the worksheet used in these sessions can be provided by email from the author upon request. The dashed lines shown on the "Incomplete Structure" image on the right side of the figure represent the missing areas at the top of the pyramid. In terms of the Mazlow model for psychological functioning, these areas represent the highest/ideal levels of functioning referred to as "autonomous".

# Pyramid Development

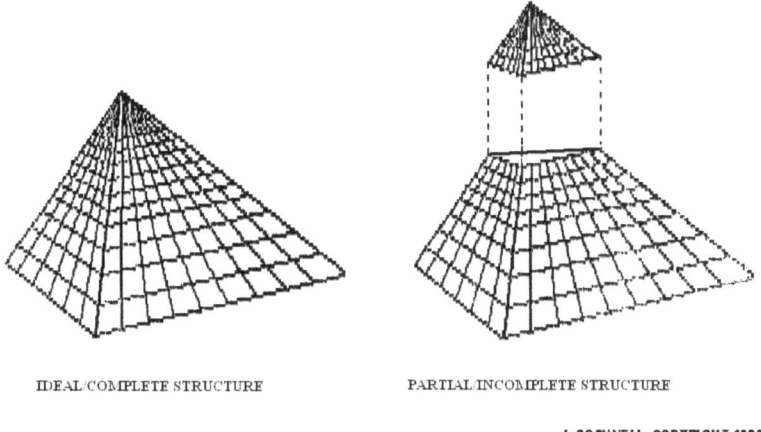

IDEAL/COMPLETE STRUCTURE          PARTIAL/INCOMPLETE STRUCTURE

**Figure A-VII-2.  Photocopy of worksheet used for the Developmental Pyramid task in treatment. (70% reduction)**

The information presented for this activity was customized to match the unique cognitive abilities of the person in a similar way as for the Path of Recovery map and treatment plan previously introduced. Also, for the juvenile to successfully comprehend and gain adequate insight about the information communicated during this activity, an interactive session length of 1.25 - 1.50 hours was necessary.

Since the specific information introduced during this session is beyond the scope of this report, only some of the key aspects developed for specifically enhancing the juvenile's emotional capacity are summarized below.

A.  The emotional development of the self takes place within the boundaries of a    structure that may be represented as a pyramid having 3 sides labeled "behavioral", "relational" and "reality".

B.  Successfully building the pyramid depends on how well the work is done block by block, layer by layer as the person grows from infancy to adulthood.

C.  Each block is put in place as the iterative result of experiences that take place within the areas making up the sides of the pyramid.

D.  The quality of block placement depends upon the choices made in dealing with the experiences in those three areas, and the quality of feedback from the 3 different sources.

The Feedback Package used in this regard is described in a separate area below.

E.  Operating at the boundary/edge of the structure is dealing with experiences in that particular area in **self-defeating ways**.

F.  Operating beyond the boundary/edge of the structure is choosing to deal with experiences in that area in **self-destructive ways**, such as using, or abusing substances. Blocks put in place in these locations distort the structure.

G.  In this model the most stable emotional and mental states are found near the ideal "balanced" operating point at the center of the pyramid for most experiences.

H.  Although incorrect, or inappropriate blocks cannot be removed, the person can develop alternative blocks by choosing to learn and practice new responses/choices for dealing with similar experiences in all areas. This was discussed as an iterative process, and consistent with Goal C of the Treatment Plan. It was very important to point out to the person and family, that because problematic blocks cannot be removed, the potential for choosing them again in the future, i.e. having a relapse, was always going to be an ongoing issue regarding the recovery process.

Since the above approach was generally too complex for understanding if presented only on an oral level to most of the juveniles in the population being served in this program, the worksheet was specifically designed as a teaching tool for use during the discussion. In practice the session was conducted by first working with the complete/ideal pyramid structure shown on the left side of the figure for introducing the basic concepts of the pyramid as a representation of the development of self, the attributes of balance, stability, and interdependence, and the importance of boundaries, personal and otherwise.

The sides of the structure were then labeled and explained in simple terms using typical examples in the juvenile's own life. This was followed by a discussion of boundaries and common examples of how each person is often found making choices that take place near the boundaries, or even outside of the boundaries under extreme experiences, or problem-solving circumstances.

Then there was a brief discussion regarding the significance of the completed structure and the concept of "autonomy" was introduced to provide some insight regarding one of the psychological **goals** of the healthy functioning adult.

Next, the presentation shifted to the right side of the figure, showing the partial structure used to represent problematic development. The reason for the missing top was explained and related to the world of adults as defined by our society. Since most of the population treated in this program had already been practicing using adult behaviors in different and inappropriate ways, all had their own examples of how they had been operating in age-inappropriate areas for a long enough period of time to have "blocks" in place there. This was often a very important treatment-related point, especially for family reintegration work. In addition, the use of inappropriate role behaviors was recognized as providing potentially serious antecedent conditions leading to substance use/abuse relapse.

Since nearly all of this population experienced problems in the area of affective management, and especially anger control, learning to deal with emotional stress using the pyramid concept was one of the most important measurable/observable treatment outcomes of that activity. This objective was accomplished by teaching a **visualization** exercise for self-help when experiencing overwhelming emotional stress/trauma. This consisted of their learning to "see" themselves in the center of their personal pyramid when becoming upset. They were taught that this was where they would be most stable, balanced, focused and, ultimately, have the maximum control over their behaviors for **coping**, making **choices** and using **alternative responses** to deal with stressful situations. Feedback from both male and female adolescents who used this technique indicated that it was very successful in that it helped them to calm themselves down and avoid negative consequences from staff. Feedback from various BCJI and AMJI staff indicated that affective management was noticeably improved for those same cases.

The above summary of a specific intervention treatment task was provided in this report to serve as an example of one successful activity developed from the use of the Esteem Therapy methodology in an insight/educational mode for applications with this substance abuse treatment model. The objectives of this treatment task/activity were to accomplish the following:

a. Facilitate important insight into the juvenile's own developmental processes.
b. Facilitate insight into the dysfunctional effects of substance use/abuse on their   developmental processes and various aspects of their life.

c. Facilitate insight into the important concept of boundaries in all areas of their life.

d. Facilitate insight into healthy vs. unhealthy emotional and mental functioning in terms of their personal pyramid.

e. Provide a visualization technique for improved affective management and emotional/mental functioning using the pyramid concept.

f. Establish the foundation for future correction of structural self-esteem defects, and growth towards new, higher levels of self-esteem.

Correction of structural self-esteem defects and growth towards new, higher levels of self-esteem became the focus of ET following the successful maintenance of the minimum level of self-esteem. Since work on other esteem-damaging issues, such as sexual abuse, etc. could affect the stability of maintaining the minimum level of self-esteem, it was prudent to perform correction first and delay the developmental work until those issues were adequately resolved.

Recognition of more general self-esteem structural defects needing correction and how to accomplish that task required a thorough understanding of the Pyramid Model and the use of ET. A description of one of the most important therapeutic treatment support tools, the Feedback Package, is given below.

## THE FEEDBACK PACKAGE

Because people with problem behaviors often have a defective system for dealing with feedback, it needs to be taken over and done for them until they are well on their way from Point A to Point B, either during their activities on the Hiking Path of Recovery, or when working with the Pyramid. Feedback given to these persons in the midst of making behavioral changes must perceive a positive "spin," or slant if it is to reinforce their continued use of new/trial behaviors. In other words, they need to hear, **"You did well,"** as much as possible when making such changes. Therefore, the feedback is orchestrated to give back the most effective information about the general features of their behavior.

The order for presenting these features is shown below.

* 1st Priority Feature - The result of their using the behaviors, i.e.

**How well the behaviors <u>worked</u>.**

\*     2nd Priority Feature - Their skill in using the behaviors, i.e.

**How well the behavior was <u>performed</u>.**

\*     3rd Priority Feature - Their effort in using the behaviors, i.e.
**How much <u>effort</u> they made.**

Giving feedback for the person's self-appraisal system, that uses these general features as if coming from each source, was made with a **script presented in ways proven to motivate** the person to continue using the new behaviors.

The script below is an example of the feedback given by a therapist, or coach to a person who just attempted using new behaviors for change. The script was meant to be followed in the exact order given, and for best results, it was worded as closely as possible to the way it is presented here:

1st Feedback Statement (From the Relationship source)

*"As I saw it, (person's name), you did well. I'm proud of you and the (result and/or skill and/or effort) of your new choice."*

2nd     Feedback     Statement     (From     the     Reality     source)

*"(Person's name), your new choice made a difference in how things turned out."*

3rd Feedback Statement (From the Personal Source)

*"(Person's name), you should really feel good about yourself for the way that worked out."*

It is important to be realistic when commenting about behavior features in the first feedback statement, because the person **knows** when the result has been bad, or their skills poor. Thus, as is often the case, the person's **effort** expended may be the only feature realistically applicable for positive feedback. Regardless of how first trials really turn out, it is very important that the person hears, **"You did well,"** from each source of feedback even if it is only about the effort that they made!

Presented in the exact order and similar wording, this **package of feedback temporarily replaces their own faulty self-appraisal system**. After perceiving, **"You did well,"** from each of these sources, if believed credible, the person unconsciously sums up all three ideal feedback statements together to arrive at a **total self-appraisal** sum equal to, **"I did well!"** A complete diagram depicting this important process is shown below in Figure A-VII-3.

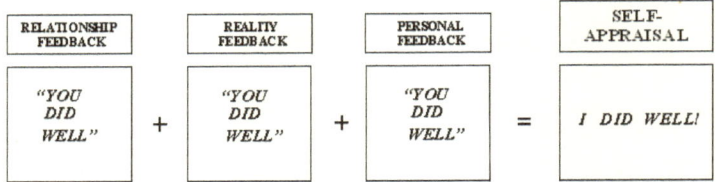

**Figure A-VII-3. The feedback summation process from the 3 sources involved in self- appraisal.**

While the first attempt at new behaviors, in fact, may not have been very good, the significance of the fact that they **risked** trying it to begin with, cannot be overestimated and must be celebrated somewhat. When someone with serious behavior problems experience <u>any</u> level of accomplishment with new choices, they usually can be motivated easily to continue using the new behaviors, if the appropriate supportive feedback is provided at the right time.

# Guidelines for Success

Complete guidelines can now be provided for giving the optimum feedback following trials of any new behaviors.

**Optimum timing** for giving feedback.

*   As soon as practical after a behavior trial has been completed.

**Optimum setting** for giving feedback.

*   A private, comfortable and informal place.
*   The individual only. No family members, friends/peers or others present.
*   No distractions, i.e. interruptions, TV, telephone calls, etc.

**Optimum behavior** for coaches and parents giving feedback.

*   Warm caring, sincere and positive. **No negatives or criticism**.
*   Informal, relaxed. Controlled voice, (friendly, warm, steady, etc.)
*   Expressive eye contact, i.e. open, friendly, caring,
*   Reflect the person's positive feelings. Be optimistic about setbacks.

Capitalize on negative experiences as "learning" opportunities.

## Basic Feedback Script

Now that the essentials have been covered, we can now present the recommended basic script to be used by coaches when giving feedback.

4.  **(Person's name), you did well.  I'm proud of you and the**

    a.   result and/or

    b.   skill and/or

    d.   effort

    **of your new choices.**

5.  **(Person's name), your new choice really made a difference in how things** turned out.

3a.  (Person's name), you should feel really good about yourself for the way things turned out.

   (or, alternative b)

**3b.  (Person's name), I bet you feel good about yourself for the way things** turned out.

Assuming things went well during a trial, the unconscious response to the total feedback would be, **"I do feel good about myself!"** After several similar trials and responses, the personal source of their self-appraisal system will be working well enough for the individual to begin using that part on their own without the need for intervention, or external prompts from the coach. It is important to point out here that, **under no circumstances** should critical, or negative feedback ever be given at this stage. In fact, when using this method, critical, or negative feedback is never appropriate – regardless of the actual trial outcome.

In the institutional setting, this method was very successful for promoting the youth's self-esteem and, as possible, various staff members were trained to use it as much as possible.

## RECREATIONAL THERAPY TECHNIQUES

Recreational Therapy was used most often with ET for the purpose of facilitating and supporting the adolescent's need for releasing emotional energy in appropriate ways and was applied during all phases and stages of treatment in the institution and the community. While working with most of the difficult issues present with this population, the feelings that were uncovered and available for release were typically "explosive" and often could not be managed by institution staff without a power struggle ensuing. If such a power struggle resulted in consequences, such as forced isolation, or worse, **4-pointing**, to restrain the person, it was this provider's experience that this caused serious destabilization/erosion of any progress made in the therapeutic goal area regarding maintenance of the minimum level of self-esteem. When these types of events occurred, the person often regressed to various self-destructive behavior choices, such as **self-cutting**, and other forms of **suicidal** ideation.

To reduce, or avert the explosive release of feelings, nearly all sessions were conducted in a 2-phase approach. The initial phase was typically held by walking around the institution grounds with the person for the first 10-15 minutes of each session while discussing difficult feelings they may have experienced since the previous session and how they dealt with them. This time was also important for ventilating feelings they had for roommates, staff, parents, etc. and any unfair treatment they perceived that needed to be processed. At this point, feelings were cognitively processed as needed but often the person required some physical, aggressive activity, such as hitting a tether ball that was available at the recreation site on the grounds.

Since many of the cases treated in this program were diagnosed as having **conduct disorder** problems, much of the substance abuse treatment work that addressed the need for improved coping skills, affective management, attitudes and perceptions, also supported their goals for improvement in that regard. It was this provider's experience that most of these problem areas could be successfully dealt with in the natural external environment.

The second phase of the session was in an office environment where more serious issues could be explored without distractions in increased depth and privacy. Since many of the underlying psychological stressors present in these cases were based on neglect, deprivation, or some form of abuse, successful resolution of these negative experiences was part of the structural correction work necessary prior to beginning to develop higher levels of esteem. Resolution of these types of issues consisted of the following approach:

- Recall and disclosure of the experiences.

- Dealing with suppressed and repressed feelings associated with their experiences.
- Working through and completing the grieving process.
- Restructuring processes.

Because the recall of these feeling issues, and the grieving process generally exposed the anger inherent to these experiences, it has been this provider's observations that the therapist must be prepared to utilize many different techniques for teaching and facilitating appropriate release, especially when the person is confined to a non-therapeutic environment. During the Institution Intervention treatment work performed on this contract, the techniques used most successfully for this purpose included fast walking, tether ball, racquetball/tennis, basketball, and billiards.

In addition to using the above recreational activities for the purpose of facilitating the grieving and restructuring process, they were also occasionally used at the juvenile's request. Since the ability to play and have "fun" in a normal way was recognized as an important developmental issue that often remained unresolved due to the introduction of substance using behaviors at a very young age, this was viewed as an opportunity for experiencing and developing personal and social coping skills in the important area of play/recreation. This was consistent with the necessity for the person's achieving balance in their recovery, and acknowledgement of the **Reality Therapy** modality that makes the important note that "fun" is a basic and important human need.

Finally, the Esteem Therapist was always receptive for engaging in play activity with a person being treated for defective self-esteem problems because, if nothing else was available, successful, fun-fulfilling play facilitated an increase in the person's self-esteem.

# ADDITIONAL THERAPEUTIC TREATMENT TECHNIQUES

Cognitive, Gestalt Reality, Psychoanalytic, Art, Educational Therapies, Hypnotherapy and Dream Analysis methods were all utilized throughout treatment, as appropriate for various purposes. Generally, none were applied in their pure forms, but only as complementary techniques in conjunction with ET. Additionally, where appropriate and compatible with this population, selected Alcoholics Anonymous/Narcotics Anonymous (A.A./N.A.) step work was used in both individual and group formats.

# THE USE OF COACHING WITH ESTEEM THERAPY

While many of the techniques used in conjunction with ET were basically derived from formal methodologies, such as Cognitive Therapy, Gestalt Therapy, etc., the technique of "coaching" was more generalized and not part of a formal category. However, this technique was important to use with ET for several reasons:

1. At appropriate times, it allowed separation from the intensive emotional nature of the treatment, while working on issues that had concrete goals and endpoints.

2. While some age groups **did** want to be told what to do and how to do it by adult authority figures, it was far more preferable to be assisted with this process by someone they perceived as a knowledgeable and credible champion of their cause. In any team activity involved with achieving specific and concrete goals, that role of being a champion is typically that of a **coach**.

3. Finally, the nature of the Esteem Therapist's relationship with the person in treatment is very similar to the **attachment/bonding** level of relationship typically found between parents and children. While this connection is very important and useful for ET treatment, when termination occurs, it is often difficult, if not impossible, to transfer this type of relationship to other appropriate figures in the person's life. However, the **coaching relationship** is one that can **be transferred** with very little training. Thus, modeling and training for parents to take over the coaching role was often a focus of family session, or individual **parenting training** sessions in the community.

In team sports and business activities, the coach's role is less critical than in the case of goals involved with psychological and behavior changes associated with obsessive-compulsive disorders. Achieving change when working with addictive behaviors based on these disorders is difficult because they involve the important dynamics of relapse, as well as recovery. As a result, the role of the coach in the kinds of cases must be defined in a different way for successful use with the psychological treatment modalities. Additionally, coaching techniques are extremely effective when used in conjunction with the Feedback Package developed for the ET modality.

# THE ROLE OF COACH IN THE ET TREATMENT PROGRAM

To be perceived as a credible coaching figure when working with psychological treatment modalities, the person does not need to be a therapist. Although it would be an advantage to have therapeutic treatment skills, it is more important for them to be perceived simply as a "reasonably" **effective functioning** adult figure. In an early book, entitled "Mental Health or Mental Illness," by William Glasser, the distinguished psychiatrist and founder of Reality Therapy, he emphasizes the concept of **effective ego** as being at the core of the highest functioning individuals in society. By this he simply meant that the person was well balanced and able to live in the most autonomous, responsible and rational manner. Of course, this is an ideal level, or goal, and one that is not achieved by everyone.

For a person to act effectively as a psychological coach, they should be perceived by the person being coached as having a reasonably high of personal functioning and, as a minimum, be at a higher level than themselves in the area of interest! In most cases, for children and even some adults, the figures in their lives that are typically perceived in this way are their teachers, doctors/nurses, clergy, and some others who are in the helping services sector of society, and with whom they have had a memorable personal experience. However, in the area of addictive behaviors, **a peer who is working successfully on their own recovery program can be an effective coach.** The skills required for the most effective coaching include the capacity for active listening and other basic communications skills that can easily be acquired by either reading or taking a course.

Because the important issue of relapse is involved with coaching persons recovering from addictive behaviors, the **characteristics** of coach must include the following:

1. Good understanding and awareness of the **appropriate boundaries** in the coaching relationship.

2. The capacity for **unconditional acceptance** of the person's responsibility and right to make their own choices, good or bad.

3. The capacity to encourage the most minute progress as success.

4. Understanding that a **single step backwards is not total failure**, and that it can be used as a learning experience.

5. The capacity to act as a guide, provide a reality check, provide honest and practical feedback and provide new options/alternatives when the person is blocked in forward movement.

It is fortunate that **learning to be an effective coach can be taught to nearly everyone**, without their being formally trained in the area of psychology, or therapeutic treatment. From this author's experience and perspective, the characteristics listed above were normal and nearly coincident with what should be typically taught for good parenting of children in general.

# Section A-VIII

## *Results And Discussion*

### PRESENTATION OF INFORMATION

General raw case data for the total population served in this program is presented in Tables I and II in Section X for reference and support of information summarized and presented in Tables III, IV and V, and Figure A-VIII-1. All tables are followed by the information that defines the specific terms used in each table. Tables III, IV and V are located at the beginning of Section X.

Table I lists gender, ethnicity, and treatment needs in the areas of substance abuse, psychiatric, emotional/behavioral and self-esteem, along with an indication of family system functionality and sex abuse history for each case.

Table II presents detailed case information for specific substances abused, treatment modes provided in this program, time since intervention treatment, time to substance abuse relapse, institution recidivism and current status.

Table III shows esteem-related treatment needs and changes for both gender and ethnicity of the population served. Additionally, this table summarizes treatment needs related to the family system functionality and history of sex abuse.

Table IV summarizes substance abuse relapse and institution recidivism data confirmed for the two primary treatment modes provided during this program.

Table V compares substance abuse relapse events and times for each case in the two treatment modes provided and supports the graphical presentation of the data shown in Figure 9.

# General Self-Esteem Results

Tables I and III indicate that the majority of the population referred to this program had serious treatment needs in all of the general categories listed by both Parole Officers (P.O.'s) and institution staff. Additionally, regardless of gender and ethnicity, a high percentage came from dysfunctional family systems and had a history of sexual abuse. The self-esteem treatment needs for this population correlated well with the treatment issues related to the family system and sexual abuse.

As reported in Table III, significant positive changes in self-esteem were observed in 88 percent of the female population treated, while 86 percent of the males treated experienced improvements. Since the Esteem Therapy model contained comprehensive developmental, emotional and victim abuse treatment components, this outcome was not unexpected.

# Substance Abuse Treatment Results

Selected details of the substance abuse history and treatment information for each case is presented in Tables II and IV. From these tables it is easily determined that the majority of the population had abused more than one substance prior to treatment. As pointed out in the descriptive summary, however, 76 percent had an alcohol abuse problem.

The two different modes of service delivery, i.e. Institution Intervention (II only), and Institution Intervention plus Community Support (II + CS) produced about the same results when substance abuse relapse and institution recidivism totals are compared.

A summary of the quantitative analysis of some of the data provided in Tables II, IV and V is presented below.

* Approximately 85 percent of the population provided institution intervention treatment services in this program **maintained some form of recovery** from substance abuse. Approximately 15 percent of this population were confirmed to have experienced a substance abuse relapse.

146

* Approximately 76 percent of the population provided institution intervention treatment services in this program **successfully remained in the community.** Approximately 24 percent of this population returned to the institution, and about 1/2 of those were confirmed to be the result of a substance abuse relapse.

* Approximately 2/3 of all full substance abuse relapse events occurred in the time frame between the first 120 to 150 days following completion of the intervention treatment phase of the program.

* Figure A-VIII-1 is a graphical presentation of the data from Table V showing the composite relapse curve from this program.

## GENERAL COMMENTS

The program reported in this special document was conducted on contract to the State of Arizona for the purpose of providing therapeutic services to a very needy population. In addition, it was planned by Purchase of Care that those services would ultimately be compared to similar services delivered by other providers for the purpose of determining the most efficacious. It was not intended by the State, therefore, to be a study program that utilized control groups and the principles of experimental design.

Although the 108 cases treated in this program over a 21 month period of time still represents a small sample size for statistically meaningful analyses and conclusions, the trend of the data acquired in this study is in excellent agreement with the trend observed in previous treatment activities performed using the Esteem Therapy model in other State of Arizona juvenile facilities, i.e. New Dawn Juvenile Institution (NDJI) for girls and Adobe Mountain Juvenile Institution (AMJI) for boys.

The most significant difference between the previous studies and the one reported in this document was the ability to follow, and have authorized contact with cases once released into the community. By this authority, their maintenance of recovery from substance abuse, or relapse was verifiable. In that sense, the II + CS (Institution Intervention plus Community Support) information may be evaluated with a high degree of validity.

While the II Only (Institution Intervention Only) data has more uncertainty inherent to it, the networking normal with this population, in conjunction with occasional informal telephone communications with the provider provided credible feedback regarding their recovery activities throughout the 21 month period. Therefore, this data may be considered as having reasonable certainty for the purpose of analysis in some areas. Since some of the results presented in the above suggest important implications and conclusions, certain facets are discussed in greater detail below.

# DISCUSSION OF SELF-ESTEEM RESULTS

The treatment needs associated with dysfunctional family systems and sexual abuse history was presented along with the self-esteem needs and treatment results in Table III as a direct reflection and recognition of their contribution as important causative factors for damaged self-esteem, as well as for the use of self-destructive behavior patterns, such as substance abuse.

As frequently pointed out throughout this document, those issues were addressed on a comprehensive basis to accomplish some resolution towards stressor reduction throughout treatment.

Although authentic changes in self-esteem can be inferred by observing many different behaviors, significant changes resulting from resolving the stresses related to the family system or sexual abuse can often only be deduced from sustained, long term improvements in the person's overall functioning following such therapeutic work. Therefore, concluding that significant changes occurred during treatment required a consensus of opinion from various independent observing sources. As indicated by the results provided in Table III, that consensus determined that those changes had been accomplished.

It is interesting to note that, although also limited in sample size, the ethnic minority juveniles and families responded very well to the self-esteem treatment provided. This result was also observed in the previous studies and is thought to be related to the emphasis on empowerment and choice that Esteem Therapy emphasizes throughout treatment.

# DISCUSSION OF SUBSTANCE ABUSE RESULTS

## Validity of Data

The substance abuse treatment results indicate that approximately 85 percent of the II + CS (Institution Intervention + Community Support) population eligible for measurement/observation were successful in maintaining a program of reduced substance use, or abstinence. Since all of these cases were followed into the community to provide services to both the juvenile and the family for supporting their reintegration and recovery, this quantitative result is considered valid.

In addition to frequent random home visits, family members were cooperative in contacting the provider if substance use was suspected. At that point, if appropriate, drug testing was performed to determine if there had been a lapse. It is important to point out that very high levels of trust and confidentiality were inherent to the therapeutic relationship established with nearly all cases to assure open, honest disclosure of violations if they occurred.

Consistent with the initial treatment plan, it was this provider's philosophy and operating procedure that a single use event, or lapse in the community could be worked through with the therapist to prevent a full scale relapse without involving anyone else. Since nearly all P.O.'s agreed with that concept and were supportive and non-interfering in those areas, the juveniles maintained a very high trust level when in the community. As a result, when lapses occurred, they felt safe enough to admit it without the fear of being returned to the institution for a single mistake. Such lapses provided a good opportunity to address issues and "high risk situations" that could not be adequately identified, nor anticipated while still in the institutional setting. Quick response for corrective action was thought to be essential to facilitate the prevention of full relapse.

The population treated in the II Only (Institution Intervention Only) service mode was not authorized for official community follow-up services or communications. However, many of these juveniles voluntarily made and maintained telephone contact for various reasons. In some cases, their reasons for continued contact was thought to be the result of a residue from the strong therapeutic/bonding relationship formed during the intervention treatment phase.

Additionally, nearly all of the population at BCJI and AMJI developed interpersonal peer relationships that facilitated networking once released. As a result of that process, the provider was often aware of details of the behaviors and activities of cases that were not directly followed for support.

For the above reasons the validity of the relapse and recovery data for this segment of the treated population was also considered to be very good and suggested the development of the composite relapse curve that is drawn between II Only and II + CS data points shown in Figure A-VIII-1.

# The 2/3 Point of Relapse

Historically, it has been found by many workers in the field of Chemical Dependency Counseling that about 2/3 of all substance abuse relapses occur within the first 90 days of treatment in most programs. This 2/3 point feature along with the slope of the relapse curve is important and will be discussed below.

An examination of the relapse event data in Table V and plotted in Figure A-VIII-1 indicates that the relapsed II + CS population experienced a 2/3 failure event point approximately 4 months subsequent to the intervention treatment phase. By comparison, the II Only population that relapsed experienced their 2/3 failure event point approximately 5 months following the completion of their intervention treatment phase.

Although limited data is available for comparison in a program of this size, the relapse difference between the two service delivery modes at the 2/3 point may be significant due to the designed difference in treatment intensity between the two modes. For those cases treated as II Only, the session variables, length and frequency, were significantly increased to provide the person with the opportunity to experience the institution intervention on a level of intensity sufficient to sustain the changes necessary to effectively maintain a substance abuse recovery program without professional community support services. The focus on greater responsibility and coping capacity for program maintenance certainly may have influenced the successful outcome apparent for this group.

This approach was conceived and applied for the purpose of solving the specific problem of how to best serve a population's treatment needs given a limited time frame without follow-on support. Evaluation of the resulting data suggests that the intensity of the institution intervention phase of treatment may indeed be effectively varied to successfully respond to those treatment needs without the use/need of professional community support activities.

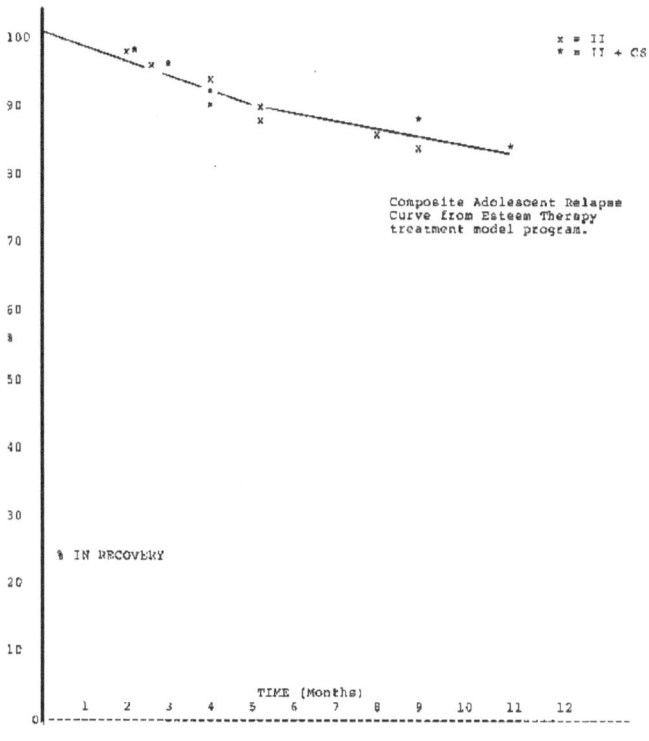

**Figure A-VIII-1. Relapse curve for the ET substance abuse treatment Program. Discrete data points represent full relapse conditions, not single lapse events.**

# Relapse Rate Reduction

Since the 2/3 point in the classical relapse curve affects the slope, and therefore the relapse rate, reflected in the initial portion of the curve, it is logical to expect that shifting that point would result in a different rate. The composite curve plotted for the data produced in this program is thought to have a radically different slope when compared with the curves for other substance abuse treatment programs.

Other program relapse rate curves are not shown here for comparison due to the fact that many measure substance abuse relapse beginning with a single lapse event. This provider does not agree with that approach. In this program, a relapse is defined as a total return to the substance use pattern that existed prior to the intervention.

It is important to note that the trend for the data generated in this program is very similar to that observed by the provider in other adolescent programs using the same Esteem Therapy substance abuse treatment model. The extent to which this trend in results is the effect of some special characteristics associated with the adolescent population is unclear at this time. However, if it assumed that the recovery results are valid, it suggests that the dynamics of the relapse process may have been altered in some way.

Although a detailed discussion of the theoretical causes for this phenomenon is beyond the scope of this report, it is interesting to speculate on the mechanism responsible for this effect. Recall that the Esteem Therapy model for substance abuse treatment requires the creation of a motivational state for commitment to the program/process of recovery. If such a state is successfully created, it is also likely that the threshold that represents the onset of failure is elevated. The presence and maintenance of that state may very well be related to an alteration in the dynamics of the relapse process simply by delaying the onset of a full return to a previous behavior pattern. Since this effect could represent a potentially significant advance in the state-of-the-art for the treatment of some addictive behaviors and populations, additional program evaluation activities that utilize the principles of experimental design are suggested for further study and verification.

# Recidivism Rate Reduction

The data summary representing the recidivism experienced by the population served in this program is shown in Table IV in conjunction with the substance abuse relapse information. Specific details regarding this aspect of treatment were not discussed, however, they are inherent to the raw case data available in Table II. The general results may be viewed as significant when compared with the predicted recidivism for this population.

The II Only population experienced recidivism of approximately 22 percent, while the II + CS population recidivism was approximately 27 percent. For both of these populations, once a case returned to the institution, this provider routinely performed a relapse assessment interview as soon as possible after arrival to determine the presenting cause, antecedent events, and substance-using behaviors. As possible, special substance testing was requested and performed for data verification. As evident in Table II, approximately 85 percent of the cases known to have experienced substance abuse relapse also returned to the institution. This is in good agreement with the historical pattern noted for the general population at the time this treatment program was initiated.

In the November 1988 State of Arizona data collected prior to this program activity, nearly all of the cases returned to the institution as a direct result of behaviors associated with their substance use/abuse. Therefore, a reduction in substance abuse relapse was expected to result in a similar reduction in institution recidivism. This phenomenon was indeed observed in previous contract work by this provider at NDJI using the Esteem Therapy substance abuse treatment model.

Compared to an average 65 percent State of Arizona juvenile recidivism rate quoted in 1987 for the Department of Corrections, as well as for the national average, the 24 percent recidivism observed for the population served in this program was significantly lower. Since most of the institution intervention services were provided at Black Canyon Juvenile Institution (BCJI), the potential financial impact associated with this reduction in recidivism was calculated using the cost at that facility during that time.

During the time period that this program was conducted the average length of confinement was approximately 4 months with a daily cost for each juvenile at $125 at BCJI. Although designed to be a 120 bed capacity facility, the average population during that time period was 65. Taking only the most accurate II + CS population data, 22 percent of the 51 eligible for this measurement, or 11 juveniles, returned following treatment. If they returned once for the minimum 3 month period in a year, the estimated cost at BCJI would have been $123,750. If the normal 65 percent recidivism figure were operating, the number returning would have been 33, at an estimated cost of $371,250. The difference of 22 additional juveniles returning would have made a $247,500 difference in cost to the state for a 12 month period, or over $433,000 for the 21 month contract period.

Using the above numerical information and the assumption that an offender only returned once each year, a minimum potential cost savings of $247,500/year was conceivably experienced as a result of the lower recidivism rate. If it were considered that the offender returned more than once each year (which has often been the case for many juveniles), that cost savings would translate into a very substantial amount for the State, and presumably, the taxpayer.

# Section A-IX

## *Summary And Recommendations*

## SUMMARY

Based on the reduced rates observed in the areas of substance abuse relapse and institution recidivism, it is generally concluded that the Esteem Therapy substance abuse treatment model program, with the addition of coaching, was completely successful and effective in achieving the goals stated in Section III, as established by the State of Arizona and the provider for the juvenile population served.

Additionally, it may be concluded from the overall success of this program that the Esteem Therapy strategy of focusing on treating the self-esteem needs in an intensive therapeutic manner with the substance abuse recovery needs of the person can result in balanced, effective functioning and improved maintenance of long term recovery. Furthermore, the addition of coaching with various aspects of ET provided an important supplement to the psychological modality. Since treating the self-esteem needs was essentially tantamount to addressing and resolving issues of development, emotional management, family dysfunction and various forms of victim abuse, it is also suggested that this comprehensive approach was validated by the success of the model applied in this program.

Of the various treatment results and accomplishments experienced in this program, several are especially noteworthy for reiteration, as they are suggestive of important findings.

* The population sample size, variety, and measurement time available in this program were sufficient to observe the long term effects of treatment using the Esteem Therapy model.

* Based on an 85 percent average sustained recovery observation for the population treated, the Esteem Therapy model provided a successful treatment program for female adolescent substance abuse.

* Since 90 percent of the female segment of the population was treated for sexual abuse issues, the Esteem Therapy model also provided successful treatment for female adolescent sexual abuse.

* The service delivery schedule for the Esteem Therapy substance abuse treatment model can be successfully varied to provide quality services for a wide range of time constraints.

* Professional community support services on a regular scheduled basis may be an unnecessary component in the recovery process using the Esteem Therapy substance abuse treatment model, given a sufficient period of time to perform **intensive intervention services in a controlled environment**.

* The institution recidivism was significantly reduced to less than 1/2 of that predicted for juveniles at state levels across the U.S. From an economic viewpoint, a substantial cost savings for State-operated juvenile facilities may be available with this program model.

* The Esteem Therapy substance abuse treatment model, in conjunction with coaching techniques, appears to have been successful in facilitating personal development in the areas of improved self-esteem and self-reliance, civic responsibility, work ethic, and to value authority.

* The substance abuse relapse dynamics appear to have been altered in a significant manner that also supports the observations of enduring change and recovery for the persons treated using the Esteem Therapy substance abuse model.

# RECOMMENDATIONS

On the basis of the overall success of this program, it is recommended that the Esteem Therapy model with coaching techniques be implemented and further evaluated in the substance abuse treatment of juveniles in other facilities. Future State-funded programs should provide for appropriate control groups in the populations served for statistical comparisons.

In addition, because the comprehensive Esteem Therapy model of recovery has been successfully applied for addressing the general recovery needs of abuse victims, it is also recommended that that aspect also be evaluated and verified for various populations in need of such services.

# THE BOTTOM LINE

Regardless of the various program and technical successes inherent to the data produced and reported for this contract activity, none can represent, nor so poignantly state the potential value of the service provided as the final juvenile seen in this program. Case #84 was a poly-addicted, Native American female from a severely incestuous reservation family system, and suffered a long history of various forms of abuse from early childhood. During the termination session, without being prompted, her simple and sensitive feelings about treatment were presented to the provider as shown in the photocopy of material in Figure A-IX-1. The right side of the figure was generated by her with the aid of a computer in a school classroom at BCJI.

That unique and personal expression of self-worth that she experienced, possibly for the very first time in her life, shows that this solitary and tragic young woman was finally able to feel better about herself. Considering her history and street-wise vigilance/defensiveness, that expression was a significant therapeutic breakthrough.

It is known that many have been helped, and other documents of similar content as this young woman's (Case # 84) have been received during the course of this contract activity. Therefore, in the final analysis, it is submitted that the simple note shown in Figure A-IX-1 alone represents the justification of this program in its entirety. There is no greater validation of this, or any other, therapeutic treatment program than the knowledge that it has helped some of the children.

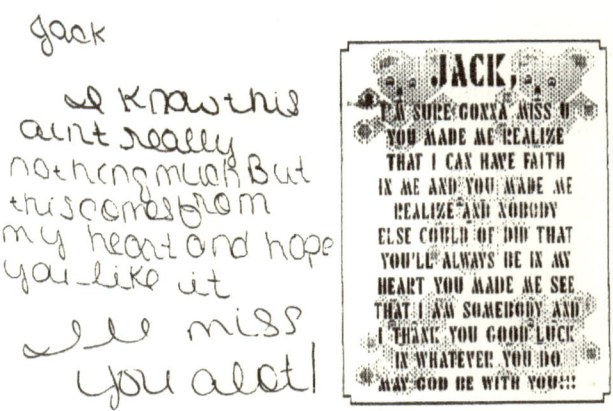

Jack

I know this aint really nothing much But this comes from my heart and hope you like it

I'll miss you alot!

**Figure A-IX-1. Photocopy of material presented at termination session of the last case (Case #84) treated in the Esteem Therapy substance abuse treatment program at BCJI.**

## POSTSCRIPT

At the completion of this program, two (2) copies of this report were mailed to each of the 50 United States for review and dissemination. The departments that received the report were the Department of Correction and the Department of Child Welfare, or Child Protective Services. Several States requested additional copies and the right to copy the report and send it to other departments. The State of Michigan had sufficient interest in the approach and results to request a workshop prior to their seeking funding for program implementation at a later date.

# Section A-X

## *Support Documentation*

This section contains important documentation supporting some of the information provided in the body of the report. The documents attached here include:

TABLE I   SELECTED RAW POPULATION CASE DATA. (PAGE 1)

| # | GENDER/ ETHNIC | SUBAB NEEDS | PSYCH NEEDS | EM/BE NEEDS | ᴖ.E. NEEDS | FAM SYS | SEX ABUSE HISTORY |
|---|---|---|---|---|---|---|---|
| 1 | F/H | H | H-BPD | H | H | DYSF | SA |
| 2 | F/W | H | M | M | H | DYSF | SA |
| 3 | F/W | H | H-BPD | H | H | DYSF | SA |
| 4 | F/W | H | H | H | H | DYSF | SA |
| 5 | F/W | M | M | M | H | DYSF | SA |
| 6 | F/H | H | H | H | H | DSYF | SA |
| 7 | F/W | H | M | H | H | DYSF | SA |
| 8 | F/W | H | L | H | H | DYSF | SA |
| 9 | F/W | H | M | L | H | DYSF | UD/P |
| 10 | F/W | H | H-BPD | H | H | DYSF | SA |
| 11 | F/W | H | H | H | H | DYSF | UD/P |
| 12 | F/B | H | H | M | H | DYSF | SA |
| 13 | F/H | H | H | H | H | DYSF | SA |
| 14 | F/W | H | M | L | H | DYSF | UD/P |
| 15 | F/W | H | H | M | H | DYSF | SA |
| 16 | F/W | H | H | H | H | DYSF | SA |
| 17 | F/W | H | H | M | H | DYSF | SA |
| 18 | F/W | M | M | M | M | F | NSA |
| 19 | F/H | H | M | M | H | DYSF | SA |
| 20 | F/W | H | H | H | H | DYSF | SA |
| 21 | F/W | H | H-BPD | H | H | DYSF | SA |
| 22 | F/H | H | H-BPD | H | H | DYSF | SA |
| 23 | F/W | H | H | H | H | DYSF | SA |
| 24 | F/B | H | M | H | H | DYSF | UD/P |
| 25 | F/W | H | H | M | H | DYSF | UD/P |
| 26 | F/W | H | H-BPD | H | H | DYSF | SA |
| 27 | F/W | H | H | H | H | DYSF | UD/P |
| 28 | F/H | M | H | H | H | DYSF | SA |
| 29 | F/H | M | H | M | H | DYSF | UD/P |
| 30 | F/W | L | M | M | H | DYSF | SA |
| 31 | F/W | H | H | H | H | DYSF | SA |
| 32 | F/W | H | M | M | H | DYSF | SA |
| 33 | F/H | H | H | H | H | DYSF | SA |
| 34 | F/W | H | M | H | H | DYSF | SA |
| 35 | F/W | H | H | H | H | DYSF | SA |
| 36 | F/H | M | L | H | H | DYSF | SA |
| 37 | F/W | H | L | H | H | DYSF | UD/P |
| 38 | F/W | H | M | H | H | DYSF | SA |
| 39 | F/W | H | L | H | H | DYSF | SA |
| 40 | F/W | H | H | H | H | DYSF | UD/P |
| 41 | F/W | H | M-S | H | H | DYSF | SA |
| 42 | M/H | M | M | H | H | DYSF | UD/P |
| 43 | M/H | H | H | H | H | DYSF | NSA |
| 44 | M/NA | H | L | L | H | DYSF | NSA |
| 45 | M/H | M | H | H | H | DYSF | UD/P |
| 46 | M/W | H | H-S | H | H | DYSF | UD/P |
| 47 | M/W | H | M | H | H | DYSF | UD/P |
| 48 | F/W | H | L | H | H | DYSF | UD/P |
| 49 | F/W | H | L | L | H | F | NSA |
| 50 | F/H | H | H | H | H | DYSF | UD/P |

# FIGURE A-X-1. PHOTOCOPY OF TABLE I, PAGE 1.

TABLE I  SELECTED RAW POPULATION CASE DATA. (PAGE 2)

| # | GENDER/ ETHNIC | SUBAB NEEDS | PSYCH NEEDS | EM/__ NEEDS | S.E. NEEDS | FAM SYS | SEX ABUSE HISTORY |
|---|---|---|---|---|---|---|---|
| 51 | F/W | H | H | H | H | DYSF | UD/P |
| 52 | F/W | M | H-BPD | H | H | DYSF | UD/P |
| 53 | F/W | M | L | H | H | DYSF | SA |
| 54 | M/B | H | L | H | H | DYSF | UD/P |
| 55 | F/W | H | M | H | H | DYSF | SA |
| 56 | F/NA | H | H | H | H | DYSF | SA |
| 57 | F/W | H | L | H | H | DYSF | NSA |
| 58 | F/H | H | L | H | H | DYSF | SA |
| 59 | F/W | H | H | H | H | DYSF | SA |
| 60 | F/B | H | H-BPD | H | H | DYSF | SA |
| 61 | F/W | H | M | H | H | DYSF | SA |
| 62 | F/W | H | H | H | H | DYSF | SA |
| 63 | M/W | H | H | lot | H | DYSF | NSA |
| 64 | F/W | H | M | L | M | DYSF | NSA |
| 65 | F/H | H | H | H | H | DYSF | SA |
| 66 | F/W | H | M | M | H | DYSF | UD/P |
| 67 | F/W | H | H | H | H | DYSF | UD/P |
| 68 | F/NA | H | M | M | H | DYSF | UD/P |
| 69 | F/W | H | M | M | H | DYSF | UD/P |
| 70 | F/W | H | M | M | M | DYSF | NSA |
| 71 | F/B | H | H | M | H | DYSF | UD/P |
| 72 | F/H | H | L | H | H | DYSF | UD/P |
| 73 | F/W | H | M | L | H | DYSF | UD/P |
| 74 | F/B | H | L | H | H | DYSF | SA |
| 75 | M/H | H | H | M | H | DYSF | NSA |
| 76 | M/W | H | M | M | M | F | UD/P |
| 77 | M/W | M | H-BPD | H | H | DYSF | NSA |
| 78 | F/B | H | M | H | H | DYSF | SA |
| 79 | F/W | H | H-BPD | H | H | DYSF | SA |
| 80 | F/W | H | H | H | H | DYSF | SA |
| 81 | F/W | H | M | M | H | DYSF | SA |
| 82 | F/W | H | L | L | M | DYSF | NSA |
| 83 | F/W | H | H | H | H | DYSF | SA |
| 84 | F/H | H | H | H | H | DYSF | SA |
| 85 | M/NA | H | L | L | H | DYSF | NSA |
| 86 | F/W | H | M | M | H | DYSF | SA |
| 87 | F/B | H | M | M | H | DYSF | SA |
| 88 | F/W | H | H-BPD | H | H | DYSF | SA |
| 89 | F/H | H | H | H | H | DYSF | UD/P |
| 90 | F/W | H | L | H | H | DYSF | NSA |
| 91 | F/W | H | L | H | H | DYSF | NSA |
| 92 | F/H | H | M | M | H | DYSF | NSA |
| 93 | F/W | H | M | M | H | DYSF | SA |
| 94 | F/H | H | H-BPD | H | H | DYSF | SA |
| 95 | F/H | H | H-BPD | H | H | DYSF | SA |
| 96 | M/W | M | M | M | H | DYSF | UD/P |
| 97 | M/W | M | M | M | H | DYSF | UD/P |
| 98 | M/H | H | H | M | H | DYSF | UD/P |
| 99 | F/NA | H | H | H | H | DYSF | SA |
| 100 | F/B | H | H | H | H | DYSF | UD/P |

# FIGURE A-X-2. PHOTOCOPY OF TABLE I, PAGE 2.

TABLE I   SELECTED RAW POPULATION CASE DATA. (PAGE 3)

| #   | GENDER/ ETHNIC | SUBAB NEEDS | PSYCH NEEDS | EM/BE NEEDS | S.E. NEEDS | FAM SYS | SEX ABUSE HISTORY |
|-----|----------------|-------------|-------------|-------------|------------|---------|-------------------|
| 101 | F/H            | H           | H           | H           | H          | DYSF    | SA                |
| 102 | F/B            | H           | H           | H           | H          | DYSF    | SA                |
| 103 | F/W            | M           | H           | H           | H          | DYSF    | SA                |
| 104 | F/W            | H           | H           | M           | H          | DYSF    | SA                |
| 105 | F/W            | H           | M           | M           | H          | DYSF    | UD/P              |
| 106 | F/H            | H           | M           | M           | H          | DYSF    | SA                |
| 107 | F/B            | H           | H           | H           | H          | DYSF    | SA                |
| 108 | F/W            | M           | M           | M           | H          | DYSF    | UD/P              |

--------------------------------------------------------------------------------

Table I Definition of terms:

    #  -  Provider's Case Number

GENDER/ETHNIC  -  Gender/Ethnicity
                  F = Female      W = White
                  M = Male        B = Black
                                  H = Hispanic
                                  NA = Native American

   SUBAB NEEDS  -  SUBAB = Substance Abuse
                       H = High
                       M = Medium
                       L = Low

   PSYCH NEEDS  -  PSYCH = Psychiatric
                       H = High
                       M = Medium
                       L = Low
                     BPD = Borderline Personality Disorder
                       S = Schizophrenia

   EM/BE NEEDS  -     EM = Emotional
                      BE = Behavioral
                       H = High
                       M = Medium
                       L = Low

   S.E. NEEDS  -     S.E.= Self-Esteem
                       H = High
                       M = Medium

      FAM SYS  -     FAM = Family
                     SYS = System
                    DYSF = Dysfunctional
                       F = Functional

SEX ABUSE HISTORY  -    SA = Sexually Abused
                       NSA = Not Sexually Abused
                      UD/P = Undisclosed/Probable

# FIGURE  A-X-3. PHOTOCOPY OF TABLE I, PAGE 3.

TABLE II   SELECTED POPULATION TREATMENT AND RECIDIVISM DATA. (PAGE 1)

| # | SUBSAB | TX | MOS SINCE I TX | RELAPSE/ MONTHS | IN... RECID | ...URRENT STATUS |
|---|--------|----|----------------|-----------------|-------------|------------------|
| 1 | A,C | I,CS | 2 | NR | NR | NSRTC |
| 2 | C,MJ | I,CS | 20 | NR | NR | 18 |
| 3 | C,X,MJ | I | 3 | NR | NR | 18 |
| 4 | A,C | I | 19 | NR | NR | 18 |
| 5 | A,C,X | I,CS | 19 | R/3 | NR | PV |
| 6 | A,C,PA | I | 20 | NR | NR | 18 |
| 7 | C,X | I,CS | 11 | R/2 | R | BCJI |
| 8 | A | I | 20 | R/9 | R | 18 |
| 9 | C,X,A,MJ | I,CS | 19 | R/4 | R | BCJI |
| 10 | C,X,MJ | I | 17 | NR | R | 18 |
| 11 | C,X,MJ | I | 21 | R/8 | NR | 18 |
| 12 | C,X,MJ | I | 20 | NR | NR | H |
| 13 | C(IV),A | I | 18 | NR | NR | 18 |
| 14 | C,A,MJ | I | 21 | R/5 | R | H |
| 15 | X,MJ | I | 17 | NR | NR | D |
| 16 | A,MJ | I | 21 | NR | NR | H |
| 17 | C,H | I | 21 | NR | NR | 18 |
| 18 | A,X,MJ | I,CS | 18 | NR | NR | D |
| 19 | A,PA | I | 20 | NR | NR | 18 |
| 20 | X,MJ,PCP | I,CS | 18 | NR | NR | D |
| 21 | C,X,MJ,LSD | I,CS | 16 | NR | NR | D |
| 22 | X,H | I | 20 | NR | NR | H |
| 23 | C,X,MJ,LSD | I | 16 | NR | NR | NSRTC |
| 24 | A,MJ | I | 20 | NR | NR | NSRTC |
| 25 | A,X,MJ | I | 21 | NR | NR | 18 |
| 26 | A,C,X,MJ | I,CS | 16 | R/4 | R | H |
| 27 | A,C,X,MJ | I | 21 | R/2 | R | 18 |
| 28 | A,MJ | I | 17 | NR | R | P |
| 29 | MJ | I | 20 | NR | NR | 18 |
| 30 | A,X,MJ | I,CS | 16 | NR | NR | 18 |
| 31 | A,C,X,MJ | I,CS | 14 | NR | R | NSRTC |
| 32 | C,X | I,CS | 16.5 | NR | NR | D |
| 33 | H | I | 16 | NR | NR | SRTC |
| 34 | A,C | I | 16.5 | NR | NR | 18 |
| 35 | A,C,X,H | I,CS | 16 | R/9 | R | PV |
| 36 | A,C(IV),MJ | I | 14 | NR | NR | SRTC |
| 37 | A,X(IV),MJ | I | 12 | R/5 | R | H |
| 38 | A,C,X,MJ | I,CS | 11.5 | NR | NR | 18 |
| 39 | C,X(IV),MJ | I,CS | 21 | R/11 | R | 18 |
| 40 | C,X,H | I | 12 | NR | NR | 18 |
| 41 | A,X,MJ,LSD | I,CS | 10.5 | NR | NR | D |
| 42 | A | CI,CS | 13.5 | NR | R | H |
| 43 | C,X,A,MJ | CI,CS | 13 | NR | R | 18 |
| 44 | A,PA | I | 11 | NR | NR | 18 |
| 45 | A,C,MJ | CI,CS | 9.5 | NR | R | 18 |
| 46 | A,MJ | CI,CS | 13 | R/1.5 | R | 18 |
| 47 | A,C | CI,CS | 12.5 | NR | NR | 18 |
| 48 | A,X,MJ | I,CS | 12 | NR | NR | 18 |
| 49 | A,C,X,MJ | I,CS | 10 | NR | R | D |
| 50 | A,C,MJ | I,CS | 9 | NR | NR | D |

# FIGURE A-X-4. PHOTOCOPY OF TABLE II, PAGE 1.

TABLE II   SELECTED POPULATION TREATMENT AND RECIDIVISM DATA. (PAGE 2)

| # | SUBSAB | TX | MOS SINCE I TX | RELAPSE/ MONTHS | INSTIT RECID | CURRENT STATUS |
|---|--------|-----|-----|-----|-----|------|
| 51 | A,C,X,MJ,R | I,CS | 10 | NR | R | H |
| 52 | A,C,X,MJ | I,CS | 8 | NR | R | H |
| 53 | A,C,MJ | I | 9.5 | NR | NR | H |
| 54 | A,MJ | I,CS | 10 | NR | NR | 18 |
| 55 | A,C,X | I,CS | 12 | NR | NR | 18 |
| 56 | A,PA | I,CS | 9 | NR | NR | 18 |
| 57 | A,X(IV),MJ | I,CS | 8.5 | NR | NR | PV |
| 58 | A,MJ | I,CS | 8.5 | NR | NR | D |
| 59 | A,C,X,MJ | I,CS | 8 | NR | R | BCJI |
| 60 | C,MJ | I,CS | 8 | NR | NR | BCJI |
| 61 | C,MJ | I | N/A | N/A | N/A | BCJI |
| 62 | A,C,X,MJ | I | 6 | NR | R | NSRTC |
| 63 | A,C,MJ,PCP | I | 6 | NR | NR | NSRTC |
| 64 | A,C | I,CS | 7.5 | NR | NR | H |
| 65 | A,C,X | I | 3 | NR | NR | NSRTC |
| 66 | A,C,X(IV),MJ | I | 3 | NR | NR | H |
| 67 | A,C(IV),X | I,CS | 6 | NR | NR | H |
| 68 | A,C,PCP,PA,MJ | I,CS | 3 | NR | NR | H |
| 69 | A,C,X,H,MJ | I,CS | 4 | NR | NR | H |
| 70 | A,C,MJ | I,CS | 5 | NR | NR | H |
| 71 | A,C,MJ | I | 5 | NR | NR | H |
| 72 | A,C,H,MJ | I | 2 | NR | NR | PV |
| 73 | X | I | N/A | N/A | N/A | BCJI |
| 74 | A,C,MJ | I,CS | 2.5 | NR | NR | H |
| 75 | C,H | I,CS | 1 | NR | NR | H |
| 76 | A,MJ | I,CS | 3 | NR | NR | H |
| 77 | A,X,LSD,MJ | I | 2 | NR | NR | NSRTC |
| 78 | A,C,MJ | I,CS | 0.5 | NR | NR | PV |
| 79 | A,C | I | 2 | NR | NR | NSRTC |
| 80 | A,X,MJ | I | 2 | NR | NR | H |
| 81 | A,MJ | I | 2 | NR | NR | NSRTC |
| 82 | A,C | I | 1 | NR | NR | H |
| 83 | A,C,X,MJ | I | N/A | N/A | N/A | BCJI |
| 84 | A,C,H,PA,MJ | I | N/A | N/A | N/A | BCJI |
| 85 | A,PA,MJ | I | 4 | R/2.5 | R | AMJI |
| 86 | A,C,X,MJ | I,CS | 1.5 | NR | NR | H |
| 87 | C | I,CS | 2 | NR | NR | H |
| 88 | A,C,X,MJ | I,CS | 0.5 | NR | NR | H |
| 89 | A,PCP,MJ | I,CS | 2 | NR | NR | H |
| 90 | A,C,X,MJ | I | 2 | NR | NR | NSRTC |
| 91 | A,C,X,MJ | I | N/A | N/A | N/A | BCJI |
| 92 | A,MJ | I,CS | 1.5 | NR | NR | H |
| 93 | A,C(IV),X,MJ | I | 21 | R/4 | R | H |
| 94 | C,X,H,PA | I | 16 | NR | NR | 18 |
| 95 | C,X,H,PA | I | 17 | NR | NR | H |
| 96 | A,MJ | CI,CS | 6 | NR | NR | D |
| 97 | A,MJ | CI,CS | 11.5 | NR | NR | D |
| 98 | A,C,LSD,MJ | I,CS | 8 | NR | NR | H |
| 99 | A,C,PCP,PA | I,CS | 20 | NR | R | 18 |
| 100 | A,C | I | 20 | NR | NR | H |

# FIGURE  A-X-5. PHOTOCOPY OF TABLE II, PAGE 2.

TABLE II   SELECTED POPULATION TREATMENT AND RECIDIVISM DATA. (PAGE 3)

| #   | SUBSAB    | TX | MOS SINCE I TX | RELAPSE/ MONTHS | INSTIT RECID | CURRENT STATUS |
|-----|-----------|----|----------------|-----------------|--------------|----------------|
| 101 | A,C,H,PA  | I  | 20             | NR              | R            | 18             |
| 102 | A         | I  | 20             | NR              | R            | H              |
| 103 | A,MJ      | I  | 20             | NR              | NR           | NSRTC          |
| 104 | A,MJ      | I  | 18             | NR              | NR           | 18             |
| 105 | C,X       | I  | 17             | NR              | NR           | H              |
| 106 | A,C,MJ    | I  | 18             | NR              | NR           | 18             |
| 107 | A,C,MJ    | I  | 18             | NR              | NR           | 18             |
| 108 | A,MJ      | I  | 19             | NR              | NR           | 18             |

Table II   Definition of Terms:

          # - Provider's Case Identification Number
      SUBSAB - Substances Abused
          A = Alcohol
          C = Cocaine
          X = Crystal Methamphetamine
          H = Heroin
          R = Robitussin
          M = Marijuana
        LSD = Lysergic acid diethylamide
        PCP = Phencyclidine
         PA = Paint
       (IV) = Intravenous injection

      TX - Treatment
          I = Institution Intervention
         CI = Community Intervention
         CI = Community Support

MOS SINCE I TX - Number of Months Since Intervention Treatment
              N/A = Not Applicable

RELAPSE/MONTHS - Substance Abuse Relapse/# of Months after Intervention
              R = Relapse
             NR = No Relapse
            N/A = Not Applicable
  INSTIT RECID - Institution Recidivism
              R = Recidivism
             NR = No Recidivism
            N/A = Not Applicable

CURRENT STATUS - Current status of juvenile
              D = Discharged from Parole prior to turning 18.
              H = Home, on parole.
          NSRTC = Non-Substance Abuse Residential Treatment Center
           SRTC = Substance Residential Treatment Center
             PV = Parole violator.  Juvenile absconded.
             18 = Person is over the age of 18
           BCJI = Black Canyon Juvenile Institution
           AMJI = Adobe Mountain Juvenile Institution

# FIGURE   A-X-6. PHOTOCOPY OF TABLE II, PAGE 3.

TABLE III  SELECTED ESTEEM RELATED TREATMENT NEEDS AND RESULTS SUMMARY.

| GENDER | ETHNIC | FAM SYS TX NEEDS | SEX ABUSE TX NEEDS | S.E. TX NEEDS | SIG S.E. CHANGES |
|--------|--------|------------------|--------------------|---------------|------------------|
| **FEMALE** | | | | | |
| | 61 W | 59 | 54 | 61 | 54 (88%) * |
| | 19 H | 19 | 19 | 19 | 17 (89%) |
| | 10 B | 10 | 10 | 10 | 8 (80%) |
| | 3 NA | 3 | 2 | 3 | 3 (100%) |
| TOTAL | 93 | 92 | 84 | 93 | 82 (88%) |
| **MALE** | | | | | |
| | 8 W | 7 | 4 | 8 | 7 (87%) |
| | 4 H | 4 | 3 | 3 | 2 (67%) |
| | 2 NA | 2 | 0 | 2 | 2 (100%) |
| | 1 B | 1 | 1 | 1 | 1 (100%) |
| TOTAL | 15 | 14 | 8 | 14 | 12 (86%) |

---

Definition of Table III terms:

ETHNIC = Ethnicity

W = White
H = Hispanic
NA = Native American
B = Black

FAM SYS TX NEEDS = Family System Treatment Needs

SEX ABUSE TX NEEDS = Sex Abuse Treatment Needs

S.E. TX NEEDS = Self-esteem Treatment Needs

SIG S.E. CHANGES = Significant Self-esteem Changes
observed during treatment.

* Notes:  Changes in self-esteem were considered "significant" when
a consensus of feedback from the juvenile, institution staff,
parents and therapist indicated sustained improvements in
identified important esteem-related areas.

The percentages calculated above reflect the total number of
cases observed to have experienced significant changes in
self-esteem divided by the total number of cases identified as
having serious self-esteem treatment needs.

# FIGURE  A-X-7. PHOTOCOPY OF TABLE III.

TABLE IV SELECTED SUBSTANCE ABUSE TREATMENT AND RECIDIVISM RESULTS SUMMARY.

| TX | TOTAL | ELIG | TOTAL #RELAPSED | TOTAL #RECID | # RECID VIA RELAPSE |
|---|---|---|---|---|---|
| II ONLY | 57 | * 51 | 7  (14%) | 11  (22%) | 6  (12%) |
| II + CS | 44 | ^ 40 | 6  (13%) | 11  (27%) | 5  (12%) |
| CI + CS | 7 | & 7 | 1  (14%) | 4  (57%) | 1  (14%) |
| TOTAL | 108 | 98 | 14 | 26 | 12 |

---

Definition of Table IV terms:

TX — Treatment Services Provided

TOTAL — Total Population Treated

ELIG — Treated population eligible for observation and analysis.

TOTAL # RELAPSED — Total number of eligible cases confirmed to have experienced substance abuse relapse.

TOTAL # RECID — RECID = RECIDIVISM
— Total number of eligible cases confirmed to have experienced institution recidivism for any reason.

# RECID VIA RELAPSE — Total number of eligible cases confirmed to have experienced institution recidivism as a result of substance abuse relapse.

II ONLY — Institution Intervention Only.
CI — Community Intervention
CS — Community Support

Notes regarding data analysis:

* — 5 cases were excluded from data analysis due to current institution status.
1 case was excluded from data analysis due to PV status.

^ — 4 cases were excluded from data analysis due to PV status.

& — 7 cases were excluded from comparative analysis due to small sample size.

# FIGURE A-X-8. PHOTOCOPY OF TABLE IV.

TABLE V    SUBSTANCE ABUSE RELAPSE RATE COMPARISONS,

| TX | RELAPSE # | CASE # | TIME TO RELAPSE | | % of TOTAL POPULATION |
|---|---|---|---|---|---|
| II ONLY | 1 | 27 | 2 | Months | 2.0 |
| | 2 | 85 | 2.5 | " | 2.0 |
| | 3 | 93 | 4 | " | 2.0 |
| | 4 | 14 | 5 | " | 2.0 |
| | 5 | 37 | 5 | " | 2.0 |
| | 6 | 11 | 8 | " | 2.0 |
| | 7 | 8 | 9 | " | 2.0 |
| | | | | | --- |
| TOTAL | | | | | 14.0 |
| | | | | | |
| II + CS | 1 | 7 | 2 | Months | 2.5 |
| | 2 | 5 | 3 | " | 2.5 |
| | 3 | 9 | 4 | " | 2.5 |
| | 4 | 26 | 4 | " | 2.5 |
| | 5 | 35 | 9 | " | 2.5 |
| | 6 | 39 | 11 | " | 2.5 |
| | | | | | --- |
| TOTAL | | | | | 15.0 |

---

Presenting the above information in graphical form in Figure 9 shows the plotting of discrete relapse data points as a function of time.

The total population eligible for relapse measurement in each treatment mode is plotted on the ordinate axis and indicates the percent (%) remaining in recovery. The time to relapse is displayed in months on the abscissa.

The time to relapse measured from the completion of the Institution Intervention phase is plotted for each case as a percentage of the total eligible population using the percentages shown in Table V.

The single relapse data point shown in Table IV for CI + CS was not used in this presentation.

# FIGURE   A-X-9. PHOTOCOPY OF TABLE V.

STATE OF ARIZONA
Juvenile/Community Services

DEPARTMENT OF CORRECTIONS
Purchase of Care Unit

Substance Abuse Services
Intervention/Community Support/Aftercare
Monthly Progress Report

Juvenile Offender: _____ K# _____ D.O.B. _____

Contractor: _____ Date of Report: _____

Parole Officer: _____

Program (Check One):

Intervention _____    Community Support _____    Aftercare _____

1. Service          Date(s) and Location of Service, i.e., institution,
   Provided (✓)      home, residential placement, office

Individual  _____    _____
Group       _____    _____
Family      _____    _____

2. Date(s) of scheduled counseling session(s) the offender did not attend.

_____   _____   _____   _____

3. Explain general progress in each area addressed in the offender's Service/Treatment Plan
   (S/TP). Indicate direction of progress by using the following code:

   ↑ Good Progress       → Marginal or No Change          ↓ Poor Progress

   S/TP Areas        Progress              Explanations

   a. _____     _____     a. _____
   b. _____     _____     b. _____
   c. _____     _____     c. _____
   d. _____     _____     d. _____
   e. _____     _____     e. _____

_____          _____
Contractor's Signature                        Date

_____          _____
Institutional Approval, If Applicable         Date

_____          _____
Purchase of Care Approval                     Date

# FIGURE A-X-10. PHOTOCOPY OF FRONT SIDE OF STATE OF AZ MONTHLY REPORT.

# Arizona Department of Corrections

1601 WEST JEFFERSON
PHOENIX, ARIZONA 85007
(602) 542-5536

**ROSE MOFFORD**
GOVERNOR

**SAMUEL A. LEWIS**
DIRECTOR

June 1, 1990

To Whom It May Concern:

During the past year it has been my great pleasure to supervise the contract provider activities of Jack Scannell at Black Canyon Juvenile Institution for females.

These activities included individual, family and group therapy/counseling services for often very difficult cases referred to him under two separate State of Arizona contracts - Substance Abuse Counseling and Psychological Counseling Services.

Although Jack consistently demonstrated good expertise with various therapeutic methodologies to successfully respond in the most sensitive manner to the needs of the client, his primary treatment and overall case management strategy was the Esteem Therapy model that he has been uniquely responsible for developing.

As a direct result of Jack's work using his model for addressing such causative psychological stressors as sexual abuse and dysfunctional family systems in addition to the presenting problem behaviors, his clients often appeared to be more higly motivated and empowered to make positive changes than previously observed.

During all of my direct staff's and my own professional interactions with Jack he consistently exceeded the requirements for an outside health care provider in all areas, especially those of documentation, procedures and team work.

In summary, Jack has been a very effective therapist and contributing member of the BCJI team, and his presence and services will be conspicously absent and missed in the future.

Sincerely,

Jocelyn Fuller, Ph.D.
Psychologist II

**BLACK CANYON JUVENILE INSTITUTION**
24601 N. 29th Avenue
Phoenix, AZ 85027

# FIGURE A-X-11. PHOTOCOPY OF LETTER FROM AZ DOC SUPERVISING PSYCHOLOGIST.

**Arizona Department of Corrections**

1601 WEST JEFFERSON
PHOENIX, ARIZONA 85007
(602) 255-5688

EVAN MECHAM
GOVERNOR

SAMUEL A. LEWIS
DIRECTOR

To Whom It May Concern:

It is with great pleasure that I write this letter of recommendation for Mr. Jack Scannell. I have worked closely with Jack in his present position as Substance Abuse Counselor, for the past two years. During this time my interactions with him have been extensive.

I have found Jack to be an excellent therapist with outstanding verbal and written skills. He always goes above and beyond what is expected of him in a therapeutic setting to assure the greatest degree of client self-learning. He is highly motivated, exhibits effective leadership skills and is able to transfer his experiential learning into a work setting for the benefit of not only his clients but his peers.

Jack displays excellent skills for effective interactions with people. His open manner, ability to listen and keen perception allows him to form solid relationships. It is because of all of these outstanding characteristics that I recommend Jack without reservation and know he will be a valuable asset to any counseling program.

Sincerely,

NICK J. Saldana
Substance Abuse Program Coordinator

ADOBE MOUNTAIN JUVENILE INSTITUTION
P.O. BOX 15800 • PHOENIX ARIZONA 85060 • (602) 869-9050

# FIGURE A-X-12. PHOTOCOPY OF LETTER FROM STATE OF AZ DOC SUBSTANCE ABUSE PROGRAM COORDINATOR.

# Arizona Department of Corrections

160¹ WEST JEFFERSON
PHOENIX, ARIZONA 85007
(602) 642-5536

ROSE MOFFORD
GOVERNOR

SAMJEL A. LEWIS
DIRECTOR

May 23, 1990

Recommendation of Mr. Jack Scannell

I am pleased to tell you of my work experiences with Jack Scannell.

He and I have worked together in several institutions of the Arizona Department of Corrections over the past four years. The last year and a half or so, we have worked together at Black Canyon Juvenile Institution. Mr. Scannell has always been a contract provider of individual and family counseling services, as well as Substance Abuse Counseling.

This man is an effective counselor. He has always established a relationship of trust with our juveniles and with their families. He is well-liked by Departmental staff and by those whom he counsels; he works cooperatively and effectively within the system. Mr. Scannell maintains a flexible work schedule, making himself available at any time to handle a crisis situation. He makes himself available to family members at their convenience.

Mr. Scannell provides services well above those called for in his contract.

All that I know of Jack Scannell, makes me believe that he will continue to be an effective counselor. I wish that money for his services could have remained in the budget.

Mrs. Josette Dobbs, CPO II

jdv: BTJS:05/23/90

**BLACK CANYON JUVENILE INSTITUTION**
24801 N. 29th Avenue
Phoenix, AZ 85027
Ph. 780-1303

# FIGURE A-X-13. PHOTOCOPY OF LETTER FROM STATE OF AZ DOC CORRECTIONS PROGRAM OFFICER.

# Arizona Department of Corrections

1601 WEST JEFFERSON
PHOENIX, ARIZONA 85007
(602) 542-5586

ROSE MOFFORD
GOVERNOR

SAMUEL A. LEWIS
DIRECTOR

To whom it may concern:

I have worked with Mr. Scannell for approximately two years and would like to take this opportunity to share with you the quality of work he performs.

As a unit staff we deal with a variety of behavioral problems. Mr. Scannell has been a very effective support system not only to staff but the youths we deal with as well. He has taken on some very difficult youths who have been in and out of correctional institutions most of their lives. Children who have had direct contact with Mr. Scannell find him to be a very effective counselor and have bonded such a trust in him it has turned around a part of their lives they never thought would come about. I have seen a youth come in to our institution with some severe problems and after receiving therapy from Mr. Scannell, walk out a changed person never to return. He is truly a team player and is very helpful to staff in helping deal with the youths on his caseload. I have had many of the children assigned to me request to start therapy with Mr. Scannell, and among the youths he deals with, he has a reputation of one counselor you can truly trust. The children feel safe with Mr. Scannell and with the trust they have in him began to open up and began dealing very sensitive issues. He is one of the most effective counselors I have seen in my fifteen years of service. Mr. Scannell is truly going to be missed by all who work with him. He has been a real asset to this institution. It is with the highest regard that I recommend Mr. Scannell in any endevors he may want to pursue.

Sincerely,
Linda Bia

Youth Service Officer

**BLACK CANYON JUVENILE INSTITUTION**
24601 N. 29th Avenue
Phoenix, AZ 85027
Ph. 780-1303

# FIGURE A-X-14. PHOTOCOPY OF LETTER FROM AZ DOC YOUTH SERVICE OFFICER.